*How to Increase Your
Sunday-School Attendance*

How to Increase Your Sunday-School Attendance

CHARLES L. ALLEN

MILDRED PARKER

Fleming H. Revell Company
Old Tappan, New Jersey

Unless otherwise identified, Scripture verses are from the King James Version of the Bible.

Scripture quotation identified TEV is from the Good News Bible—New Testament: Copyright © American Bible Society 1966, 1971, 1976.

Library of Congress Cataloging in Publication Data

Allen, Charles Livingstone,
   How to increase your Sunday-school attendance.

   1. Sunday-schools—Growth   I. Parker, Mildred,
joint author.   II. Title.
BV1523.G75A44   268   79-22655
ISBN 0-8007-1088-6

CONTENTS

Appendixes

PREFACE

In September, 1968, Mrs. Mildred Parker became a member of the staff of the First United Methodist Church in Houston. About the second week she was here, she told me that we needed to paint the nursery. I innocently said that Mr. Ed Reichert, an architect in our church, would be glad to help select the colors and give advice.

To make a long story short, painting that nursery was the beginning of a renovation program in this church which cost a total of three million dollars. One thing led to another, until the entire building was completely rebuilt. However, it was the best money the church could have ever spent. Money spent to make God's House attractive is never wasted. The same people who give to build God's House also give to the great mission causes of the church.

The First Methodist Church is located in the downtown section of Houston. For more than a hundred years, this church was noted for its pulpit ministry. As we began our building-renovation program, we also emphasized our Sunday-school program. The pulpit program has not decreased: in fact, we are having larger attendance at the worship services than we have ever had. We have duplicate morning church services—one is on television and the other on radio.

We have learned that promoting the Sunday school also promotes church attendance. Mrs. Mildred Parker, as the diaconal minister of Christian Education, has given direction and leadership to the Sunday-school program. I, and the other ministers on our staff, support the program both from the pulpit and in active service. Each of the ministers of our church regularly teaches a Sunday-school class.

During the time we have renovated our building and have been emphasizing our Sunday school, our Sunday-school enrollment has increased to 4,000 members.

In the pages of this book, we outline the principles we have used and ideas we have observed in the programs of many other Sunday schools.

Working full time on Mrs. Parker's staff are Miss Mary Frances Allen, assistant director of Christian Education; Mrs. Patsy Thornton, director of Children's Ministries; Mrs. Jeannie Whitehurst, director of Youth Ministries; and Mrs. Judy M. Saenz, administrative assistant in Education.

We especially express appreciation to Mrs. Judy M. Saenz for valuable assistance in preparing this manuscript.

CHARLES L. ALLEN

How to Increase Your
Sunday-School Attendance

1

As the Sunday School Grows, So Grows the Church

There has never been a growing church that did not have a growing Sunday school. This statement is extreme, and we are sure that there are exceptions, but we are also sure that the percentage of exceptions would be very small. We do not believe that there is even an average of one growing church out of a hundred that does not have a growing Sunday school.

We have seen churches grow for a time because of the popularity of a pastor, or maybe because of an extremely fortunate location; but, over the long run, the growth of the church is almost without exception the result of the growth of the Sunday school. Certainly all of us who have worked very long in the church would readily agree that the quickest way to build the church is to build the Sunday school.

We, the authors of this book, currently work together as the director of Christian Education and as the pastor of a church located in downtown Houston, Texas, with a membership of 11,500. Each of us has served small rural churches, county-seat town churches, suburban city churches, and large downtown churches.

Our observations, however, go far beyond the churches in which we have actually served. One or the other of us has had opportunities to teach training classes in various churches over the country, hearing directly from laypersons involved, talk with large numbers of pastors and other staff persons responsible for Christian Education in various circumstances, attend and participate in numerous conferences relating to all phases of Christian Education in the local church. Combined, we have had many years of experience and the opportunity of learning from the experience of others. We have discovered several basic and evident principles in relation to the Sunday school.

The Pastor's Attitude

We believe that the attitude of the pastor is almost the controlling factor in whether or not a Sunday school grows. If the pastor is only concerned about the worship services, pastoral duties, and administrative responsibilities, and fails to give attention to the promotion of the Sunday school, it is almost certainly not going to grow. On the other hand, regardless of the size of the church or the location or any other condition, if a pastor really wants the Sunday school to grow, it can and will grow.

The pastor cannot do it alone but can be a powerful motivator. The pastor must plan with leaders. The congregation needs to know that the pastor considers Christian Education to be important. The main question that needs to be asked within any church is, "Do we want our Sunday school to grow?" If the answer to that question is, "Yes," then the Sunday school will grow. On the other hand, if the pastor and the people of a church are smug and satisfied and are reaching as many people as they want to, then they are certain not to grow. Many churches adopt a defeatist attitude, and then they *are* defeated.

The Attitude of Other Staff Workers—Professional and Volunteer

A professional Christian educator, when there is one on a church staff, can do much to assist the pastor and the people of the church in increasing attendance in Sunday church school. That person should, with the pastor, be a motivator, as well as an enabler and an encourager. The professional Christian educator is not to do the work of the people, robbing them of the joy of exercising their discipleship, but should lead them and be personally supportive as they perform their duties. He or she should be concerned with the total ministry of the church and can do much to insure the harmonious interlocking of the various facets of the church's ministry. This affects attendance in a positive way.

Let it be emphasized that dedicated volunteers can do more than is dreamed of to get things going in a positive, rewarding way. Those persons can work very closely with the pastor and other staff. In every church there are keen, talented Christians who have great abilities. Usually, it is their pleasure and joy to use these in the service of their church. Those volunteers should read the denominational materials of the church, and should regularly participate in leadership enterprises. Most of the responsibility of the Sunday church school falls on the volunteer.

The important question for any committee, pastor, teacher, leader, or director of Christian Education to ask is, "Do I really want a bigger school?" Unless you're willing to ask the question and answer it affirmatively, you're already defeated. There are some churches which are so ingrown that they do not want the responsibility of additional persons. Others feel hopeless and believe that the situation cannot be changed. They have given up, thinking there is nothing they can do. They have a defeatist attitude.

Once a church decides it wants to have a larger school, the next step is to decide it can. A positive belief in the idea is important. Any Sunday school can increase its enrollment and attendance, if it believes it can and is willing to work at it. Just wanting it to happen is not sufficient, but the faithful application of the principles in this book will bring visible results.

Numbers or Quality?

Perhaps you have heard the statement "we are not interested in numbers; we are interested in quality of education." That statement is made as if numbers and quality are in contradiction to each other. Actually the opposite is true: Numbers usually produce quality. Also, quality produces numbers; either way the result is growth. Usually the person who says, "I am not interested in numbers" is using that as a defense mechanism.

To say we are not interested in numbers is both unwise and unchristian. In the New Testament, there is a story, which came from the lips of our Lord Himself, about a shepherd who had 100 sheep. He did not say he had *some* sheep. The shepherd knew the exact number. Not only that—every night he counted his sheep. Then, one night, one sheep was missing, and he went out that very night to find the missing sheep. Many other incidents can be cited in the New Testament when numbers received attention.

The question is, "Numbers of what?" In talking about the Sunday school, we are talking about numbers of babies and little children and adolescents and older youth and young adults, both single and married, and middle-aged people and older people. The word to use really is not *numbers* but *people*. In the church we are interested in people.

It is true that quality is important. Quality helps to get

persons, and it helps to keep them once you have them. Poor organization, poor teaching, lack of friendliness and concern are all signs that quality is lacking. But quality is of no avail unless there are persons who will benefit by it. We need to remember that it is for persons that the church exists. The church is an avenue for God's love and concern, a way for persons to be brought into right relationship with Him.

When the pastor and the people of the church decide they are interested in people—interested in winning them to become informed, intelligent Christians, interested in learning more about the Bible, interested in bringing them into the life of the church, interested in challenging them to make everyday decisions harmonious with God's will for their lives, interested in making people effective in the building of the kingdom of God on earth—when these become their interests, the Sunday school begins to grow. The church attendance grows. The financial support of the church grows. The missionary concern of the church grows. The witnessing power of the church grows. In fact the words of our Lord ". . . I will build my church . . ." (Matthew 16:18) become a reality in that church.

There Are People Who Need the Sunday School

We need to remind ourselves that two-thirds of the people in most communities are not in any Sunday school anywhere. There are at least 130 million people in the United States who are not receiving any formal religious education of any kind. Every church in America is located in the very center of a great mission field. A portion of the people in our country receiving no religious education is living in the parish of any church and is the responsibility of that church. We repeat, any Sunday school, anywhere, in spite of any condition, can grow if it really wants to.

Growth in Church Membership

Growth and membership in the church are directly related to growth in the Sunday school. There are two reasons for this:

1. Children and youth who grow up regularly participating in the Sunday school are more likely to have a love and loyalty for the church, and, at some point commit their lives to Christ in church membership. Also, as adult classes reach out and bring in new members, those new class members find that they want to belong to the church. On the other hand, there are those who join a church. Perhaps they are attracted to the church by the worship service. If these persons are led into membership of a Sunday-school class, there is a far greater chance that they will remain members of the church. One can attend the worship service of a church for many years and not become acquainted with anyone or make any friends. This is not so in a Sunday-school class. There one becomes a part of a fellowship that binds persons to each other and together to the church.

2. In years gone by, churches learned that evangelistic meetings and visitation evangelism brought new members into the church, but did not always hold them. The Sunday school is the great conserver of church members.

Frequently it happens that if one member of the family, be it father, mother, youth, or child, is recruited into a class, that one member will bring the remainder of the family into other classes. The Sunday school not only becomes the best evangelistic agency of the church, the members of the Sunday school also become involved in the church. As a rule, these persons have a growing faith and commitment and are a part of the activity of the church. They become not only good people but good for something within the church. Such persons usually remain as productive members of the church. They are not here today and gone tomorrow.

The school of the church is a powerful means of recruitment for church membership. Assimilation into the total life of the church is done more effectively through it. A church member who is involved in the church's Christian Education ministry is more likely to stay with the church and render service in and for the church.

Church Attendance

An important fact to remember is that the attendance at worship services is very closely tied in with the attendance at Sunday school. There are some churches in which a large number of the Sunday-school people go home and do not stay for church, but really those are rare cases. The larger the Sunday school, the larger the worship attendance. There will always be some persons who want to attend just the worship service and others who want to attend only the Sunday school, but the fact remains: Sunday school and worship attendance go hand in hand. The two rise and fall together. There is a close relationship between the two.

One of the responsibilities of the leaders of the Sunday school is to teach appreciation for the total ministry of the church. This will promote loyalty and a desire to participate fully. If a substantial number of persons attend Sunday school and do not stay for church, somebody in the Sunday school has grossly failed. Wise are the teachers, officers, and leaders who see the importance of being present in the worship service and who teach loyalty and support of that aspect of the church. Wise, also, is the minister who, from the pulpit, speaks in loving, building terms about the Sunday school and who gives thoughtful attention to its promotion.

A spiritual, unifying force will be present when proper emphasis is placed on both Sunday school and worship service. Together, they lead persons into commitment and discipleship for our Lord.

Finances

The finances of the church pretty well parallel the attendance at the church. Increasing Sunday-school attendance increases giving and increases the opportunity of the church to meet its own needs, as well as its outreach missionary opportunities and responsibilities.

We are all familiar with the persons whose names are on the roll of a church who say, "I do not attend, but I contribute." There are some persons like that, but they are a very low percentage of the church. And a very small part of the church's budget comes from people who do not attend. The fact is that the people who support the church with their giving are the same ones who support it with their presence. When persons stop coming to church, usually they stop contributing in any other way: money, time, service.

Persons who are enrolled and regularly attending Sunday school and worship services feel a responsibility because they are on the inside, in the pulsebeat of the great body. They are a functioning part of the body. Somehow, God's demand upon their lives becomes more real. The joy and release of response is a shared thing.

A good Sunday school more than pays for itself. Church leadership which invests generously in supporting, building, and maintaining a good Sunday school will reap rich dividends through the stewardship of its members.

Wise churches realize that a financial campaign should be preceded by an attendance campaign. And the best place to begin that attendance campaign is in the Sunday school.

So let us sum up what we have sought to say in this chapter. A growing church has a growing Sunday school. Sunday-school attendance can be increased; this is true of any church, anywhere, under any conditions. The church grows as the Sunday-school attendance grows; conversely, church membership declines as the Sunday school declines. Church finances increase in direct proportion to attendance increase. Stewardship in service becomes more evident. The church is enabled to be and do.

2

The Way to Begin

Do four simple things which should motivate you to use
the Sunday school as an avenue for ministry:

1. Make an attendance chart of the Sunday school for
the past several years. This is a good barometer of the
health of the church. If your record is good, you can do
better. If it's poor, it doesn't have to be that way.

2. List the names of those who have united with the
church during the past twelve months and determine how
many of them came from the Sunday school. Two or three
generations ago, the majority of this group would have
come out of special evangelistic efforts, such as a revival.
This is not so today. Some studies show that at least two-
thirds come from the Sunday school. Giving one's life to
Christ is a normal response to Sunday-school participation.

3. Without naming names, so no one will be embarrassed, list how many persons who are members of the
Sunday school contribute to the budget and how many are
not contributing to it. You will be surprised at the larger
percentage of the Sunday-school members who are givers.
If nothing else sells the church on the value of the Sunday
school, this will do it!

4. List the persons who are doing things in the church:
those who can be depended on to carry out the tasks of
ministry, whether the tasks be large or small. Generally,
these persons will be involved in Sunday school.

Find the Prospects

You see some real possibilities in the Sunday school! You're ready to make things happen through it! You would like to make it grow! Take these additional steps:

Make a survey of the entire congregation to determine who is and who is not being reached through the Sunday school. One way is to use the membership roll of the church and from that list make family cards, listing heads of households and family members, where this applies. Indicate the age category of each person. Show name of class to which each person belongs, or show lack of membership in a class.

```
┌─────────────────────────────────────────────────┐
│                           Date: _____          │
│    Family name: _____  │
│              Mr.   _____  Class: _____     │
│              Mrs.  _____  Class: _____     │
│              Miss  _____  Class: _____     │
│    Children          Age:     Class:              │
│    1. _____   __ __ __ __ __ __ __            │
│    2. _____   __ __ __ __ __ __ __            │
│                                                   │
└─────────────────────────────────────────────────┘
```

Place these cards alphabetically in a file and keep them updated as the Sunday-school status of persons changes. Use them initially to compile a prospect list for recruitment into the Sunday school. You will be surprised at how many new-person possibilities you will find. If you don't get them the first time, you have their names and may try them later.

An added bonus is that you have a record showing where a class member may be found at any given time. You have a card on which may be recorded such things as special needs, special talents, known interests. One church uses these cards as a source for collecting data for the recruitment of teachers, even recording on them responses and promises. For example, Mrs. Jones might say, "When my baby is older, I will teach." Your card would indicate this, and read, "Call on Mrs. Jones at such and such a time." When that time comes, again invite Mrs. Jones to teach.

Perhaps your church already has a Cardex system for recording members. Sunday-school membership may be indexed into these and used very similarly to the family-card system. One large church which has this system double-checks it annually and lists Sunday-school prospects to be called or visited. That particular church has had success in designating an evening in which to bring together representatives from each adult class for the purpose of doing mass calling. They secure from the local telephone company the use of operator phones which are located in one huge room. Two hundred persons may call at one time, using a prospect card, on which has been recorded information from the master card.

Such a plan means that prospects are assigned to certain classes. However, each caller has a fact sheet on other classes and other functions within the church so that a referral may be made, when it seems pertinent. There is additional follow-up by each class, with a warm welcome ready for those new persons enrolled in the class or persuaded to visit.

Often, callers discover family situations which need the attention of the church. Usually, persons are very happy to hear from someone else in the church, particularly if the caller is interested in *them*. Even if the call does not get a new Sunday-school member, it will have been a contact. And that's good when done in the right spirit.

The important thing is to adopt some workable plan which will keep you informed about Sunday-church-school prospects within your local congregation.

Take a good look at your neighborhood and the surrounding area from which you might recruit Sunday-church-school members. Who are the target people out there? What are their ages? What are their circumstances? What are some of the needs which may exist?

Where are these people? Population shifts may have occurred. You may have to extend your search to farther boundaries, or you may have to focus in on a new housing project, an apartment complex, an urban community, or a scattered rural settlement. But the people are there. We would venture to say that, without exception, in every area, we can find those who are unchurched.

Begin keeping a record of those who visit your church and your Sunday church school. Adopt a plan to contact these persons after they have visited. Become acquainted with them. Let them know you are glad they visited. Invite them to join you. Find out whether or not their needs and interests were met.

One church has designated persons who do telephoning of visitors. Another church writes each visitor and encloses a feedback form, inviting a response from him or her. Another church has a church visitor (this could be several persons) who goes to the home of the one who has visited.

Decide What You Would Like to Do

You see some possibilities for finding people. What's the next step in beginning?

Effective, successful Sunday schools have a sense of purpose. They have a reason for existing. It is revitalizing and motivating for persons to think together about these purposes, and to state them in some concrete, concise way.

The pastor, other key staff persons, if these exist, leaders in the church, and representative persons from the congregation should be involved. Existing classes, including children's groups, could be involved in stating what they believe the church is called to be in its Christian Education ministry. A group such as the Christian Education Council could pull all the statements together into one unifying statement of purpose which the whole church adopts.

Next, through your education council, or whatever your planning group may be called, set down some broad statements of what you would like to do. These are called objectives. Since we are considering the primary task of increasing Sunday-school attendance, your number-one objective would be just that. In addition, you might list such things as providing more adequate facilities, finding a better way to recruit and train and sustain teachers and other workers, or the means of introducing and developing the use of effective denominational resource materials. Your objectives should be reflective of your needs and your purposes.

Develop a Plan of Action

It's important to come to a decision on some specific goals which are attainable within a given time span. For example, one goal might be, as we've already outlined, the complete survey of the existing congregation to find prospects for Sunday school. Set a time limit within which this is to be done. Then, another goal could be contacting these persons. Again, set the time span within which this is to be completed.

Other goals, or statements of what you intend to do, would be formulated in accordance with what you would like to do. Remember they should be feasible. For example, if a desirable objective is to provide more adequate facilities, your goal may be to study existing space and reassign it in a more equitable way. The building of new facilities might or might not be a realistic goal.

At any rate, together, develop a plan of action. If many persons are involved in this from the beginning, there will be excitement and motivation. Things will happen if you will follow these simple steps. Do not bypass them. The chapters ahead give insight as to how to put meat on them. Get started! Begin now.

Use Evaluation as a Tool

Evaluation of what you are already doing should be a ready tool all the way through your planning and implementation process. You will affirm much of what you are already doing. Some things you will not want to change. But some things may no longer be serving a good purpose. From time to time we need to look honestly and realistically at what is happening. What you are trying to do is to formulate a launching pad for courses of action. Evaluation and reevaluation in a systematic, measurable way are wonderful tools to use in gaining and keeping persons in Sunday church school!

3

Open the Front Door Widely, but Close the Back Door Tightly

We can get so concerned about getting new members into our Sunday school that we forget about keeping them once we get them. The result is that our members can go out the back door as fast as they come in the front door. The leadership of every church must look for the leaks in its membership. Why do people come in the first place? That is an excellent question. An equally important question is: Why do they quit coming?

Is it possible that natural increases are being offset by regularly occurring losses? Any school would have some natural increase as children are born into families or new families in the area put their membership in to the church. At least there will be some visitors who are potential Sunday-school members. Often, this natural increase is undermined by unnecessary, regularly occurring losses.

If the drainage is equal to or greater than the input, the result is a school without any increase or a school in which attendance is steadily dropping.

Perhaps you have had a car tire which would go flat over and over. The attendant at the gas station would fill it with air, but all the air would leak out slowly, and the tire would go flat again. There was a flaw in the tire! The same principle applies to our Sunday school. There may develop flaws or weaknesses which will cause losses that prevent any gain in attendance. *We need to identify the flaws.* Once these are recognized and corrective measures are applied, a healthily functioning school will exist. People will gladly come to it and remain in it. It will count for something in the lives of people. It will become a means of influence beyond itself.

True, there are sometimes circumstances beyond anyone's control, but, before giving them careful evaluation, a school should not accept these as being absolute. Creative minds put to work can usually find a way around the circumstances.

Identify Causes of Losses

Let us look at some of the reasons we lose our Sunday-school members:

The Teacher Problem.   Without any doubt, a most significant factor in the success of a Sunday-school class is the teacher of the class. God has always worked through personalities, and the Sunday school is no exception. A teacher who gives evidence of loving concern for the members of a class, who presents thoughtful and helpful material, and who stimulates the class to participate in discussion, will build and hold a class. A teacher should be selected, recruited, and commissioned to teach a particular group for a designated tenure. The rotating of teachers from Sunday to Sunday is never as effective as having regular teachers. Team teachers, who plan and teach together, add strength, especially in children's and youth classes. The church that allows a class to meet without a regular teacher or leadership will soon lose that class.

It naturally follows that a teacher who is irregular or does not seriously prepare the lesson or who does not show interest in the members of the class will see the class quickly decline. On the other hand, interest and attention on the part of a teacher results in better attendance on the part of the class members.

There are some teachers who are great in one class and who are misfits in another class. Here, it is the responsibility of the leadership of the Sunday school in the church to watch for these misfits and stop putting square pegs in round holes. Make changes as needed. Some teachers who do a marvelous job with children would fail with youth and adults. Others know how to relate with youth, and still others with adults. Get the teachers who can relate with the classes with which they are working. Just because a teacher is not successful in one class does not mean that teacher should be discarded and not used some other place.

Inadequate Teacher Training.   One of the most important things a church can do is to discover those persons who are potentially good teachers and provide them with opportunities to grow and learn. It's a beautiful thing to see a person unfold—to be on fire, so to speak, with the passion of learning, sharing, and enabling others to experience the meaning of the Christian faith.

In other words, teacher training and nurture are musts. Subsequent chapters go into this more fully. At this point we need to remember that the teacher is a vital link to opening the front door widely and closing the back one tightly.

Teachers need to become pupils from time to time. As pupils, they get a new and fresh look at what teaching and learning is all about. In every Sunday school, there should be vacations and study leave for teachers. In addition, there should be an ongoing leadership-development program. Teachers who know their responsibilities, who are growing persons themselves, can do much to shut that back door while holding the front one wide open. Some suggestions on this are given in chapter six.

Lack of Purpose or Mission.   Another cause for losses is

having a Sunday school that does not have a purpose or mission. The mission of a Sunday school is to enable persons to become Christians and to equip them to live Christian lives. To do this, we need to have Christlike relations, to be patient, forgiving, and loving. Too many times there are quarrels and misunderstandings and unchristian attitudes and actions in the Sunday school. The Sunday school that does not exhibit the Christian spirit is not going to hold its members.

Inner Frictions. Because there are so many opportunities for differences to develop in a church, it is a wonder that any church survives. A church can become divided over such things as the popularity of the pastor, the quality of the choir, whether or not to build a new building, or theological attitudes. We know of one church in which it became a serious matter of dissension over whether or not to paint the nursery light pink or light green. That seems silly, but such things really can happen. In fact the unhappiness which develops in many churches is usually over some small, insignificant thing. Whatever the reason, when a church begins to develop inner tensions and unhappiness, then unchristian attitudes and actions develop and—in direct proportion—loyalty, support, and attendance decrease.

Sunday-school leaders need to be very aware that their first duty is to present the Christian spirit in their attitudes and in their lives. There are some things that are just not worth differences of opinion. Better to let some issues go than to let some persons go.

Sloppy Organization. Another cause for the back door of many Sunday schools being left open is sloppy organization.

Organization is that procedure which defines, among other things, how many classes there will be, where the classes will meet, who the membership will be, and how and when leadership will be enlisted and trained. Through organization, there is a plan to be followed. Certain officers with due responsibilities are appointed or elected. Time schedules are determined. Provisions are made for record-keeping and for the use of records in keeping in touch with persons. Persons are assigned the responsibility of welcoming visitors and escorting them to classes, and there is a follow-up plan in each class. A procedure for selecting and providing literature, aids in teaching, and equipment is part of organization. Each class within the total church school must have a harmonious, cooperative mode of operation so that all parts finally fit together. We must remember that:

> We have many parts in the one body, and all these parts have different functions. In the same way, though we are many, we are one body in union with Christ, and we are all joined to each other as different parts of one body. So we are to use our different gifts in accordance with the grace that God has given us . . . .
>
> Romans 12:4–6 TEV

All these procedures, and others, make for a more smoothly operating Sunday school which will attract and keep persons. It frees persons.

Just like any other organization, a Sunday school has certain rules to follow. It should begin on time, and it should quit on time. There should be some obligations placed upon the student in the Sunday school. Lessons should be studied. Places of service should be given. Every pupil should feel needed as well as wanted.

Above all we need to remember that poor, inadequate, bad teaching and bad, weak religion are worse than no teaching and no religion.

Weak Study Plan.   Use of study materials irrelevant to the lives of persons turns them away. From time to time, there should be an opportunity for class members to express their interests and needs so that appropriate studies may be set up to meet these.

Studies of the Bible, church history, and theological beliefs are basic. However, a well-rounded curriculum plan will include opportunities to explore these in relation to family life, to world conditions, to mission, and so forth. Almost without exception, any Sunday school should use the literature provided by its own denomination. In the long run this is the best procedure. The Sunday school that begins to use another type of literature eventually loses. We strongly recommend the literature of the denomination.

Unfriendliness. According to a recent survey, the number-two contributing factor to Sunday-school dropouts (poor teaching being number one) is lack of friendliness on the part of class members. Classes may become exclusive little clubs. Members tend to love and appreciate each other to the point where they forget others, and a newcomer feels left out. Some groups become so self-sufficient in their own fellowship that they do not want to grow.

Poor Facilities.   Another reason persons go out the back door is through a lack of classroom facilities. In some churches there is not a suitable room available for a class. There really is no excuse for this. Any church can provide the facilities, if it really wants to. There are always those who shout out, "We are not able to build more facilities or to renovate what we have." This is not the case. The church is able to do it, and the church needs to be stimulated to provide the physical necessities for a successful Sunday school. Across the years we have watched it, and we have discovered that no class will remain larger than the room provided will comfortably care for. It may be that for a little while an overcrowded classroom will stay overcrowded, but eventually the attendance will drop to the reasonable physical capacity of a room or a building.

At this point we need to remember that there are always some who will say, "It is a shame to spend that much money on a room that is going to be used only one, or maybe two, hours a week." The answer to that is, "Those one or two hours are the one or two most important hours of the week for those who use that room."

However, let us again emphasize the fact that new and beautiful buildings and equipment do not in themselves secure large Sunday-school attendance. The truth of the matter is that the tendency is the opposite: We can get so interested in our facilities that we forget to bring in new members. Buildings do not bring members. It is workers who bring members. But the physical building and the equipment for the Sunday school are very important, and let it be laid on the conscience of the church to provide facilities for the teaching of the Christian faith to as many people as possible. Properly used, the building may be a tool to win persons to Christ and to developing persons, Christian motives, attitudes, and actions.

Lack of Commitment to Christ.   The main reason people go out the back door of a Sunday school is that they are not won to commitment to Christ in the Sunday school. Let us never forget that the purpose of the Sunday school is to lead persons to commit their lives to Christ. The Sunday school is not a communion of saints; it is a school for sinners. Oftentimes we think of the Sunday school as a place to send children and youth, and truly it is; but the Sunday school is also a place to win adults for Christ. Certainly, it is that place which can equip all for discipleship.

The ignorance of adults—both in and out of the church—about the Bible is really appalling. Recently, in an adult group of church members numbering 106, slips of paper were passed out; and the members were asked to write down who went up on the mountain and wrote the Ten Commandments. Twenty-eight of the number did not write the name of Moses. In another church group of about thirty people, ten did not know whether the Book of Revelation is in the New Testament or the Old Testament. We take for granted that our people know a lot more than they do know. The disconcerting fact is that many church members are appallingly ignorant about the Bible and about the real meaning of the Christian faith.

Yet being a Christian is the most thrilling experience of life. The Sunday school that wins persons to Christ is the one that keeps them from going out the back door and has new workers and new enthusiasm.

The Sunday school that makes Christians is a growing Sunday school. The Sunday school that does not develop Christians is going to die and deserves to die.

For You to Do

Let us suggest some definite projects for the leadership of the Sunday school. Prepare to close that back door. Plan to open, even more widely, the front one.

Go over the rolls and write down the names of those who have quit attending in the last year. Some of these have moved away. Some have joined other churches, but some have just quit. Go to the trouble to find out why they quit.

Ask yourself the question, "If those who had not quit had stayed with us, what would our Sunday-school membership and attendance be today?"

Reexamine the methods in your Sunday school and church in selecting, supervising, training, and rotating teachers. Then ask yourself, "Are we doing the best job, at this point, that we could be doing?"

Let the committee you select ask and answer such questions as: Are we using the best of study materials? What can be done to make the building best serve its purpose?

Does our Sunday school begin and close at the appointed times? Is reverence for the building and facilities promoted? Is there evidence of joyous participation so that there are no discipline problems? And, mainly, is our Sunday school developing Christians? We need to face honestly the question of whether or not it really makes any difference in the lives of people who attend our Sunday school. If no difference is made in their lives, we need to make a difference in our Sunday school. And we need to determine the differences we need to make.

One of the most thrilling things that can happen is for a group of the leaders of any Sunday school to sit together and give a personal testimony of how the Sunday school made a difference in his or her own life. Then ask the question: "Are those differences being made in our Sunday school today?"

In short, really do an evaluation, or study, of your situation. Define a purpose for your church, set realistic goals, and get to work!

4

Where We Are Weak, We Can Be Strong

Every person has strengths and weaknesses. Many times, in overcoming weaknesses, a person reaches his or her highest peaks. The same thing can be said about a Sunday school. Really our weaknesses can be our greatest assets if we will do two things: Find out what those weaknesses are and do something about them. Any one of us who has worked in the Sunday school can make a list of possible weaknesses. Such a list would include the teaching staff, the literature, the record keeping, regular efforts to get new members, follow-up on absentees, the attractiveness of the building, how interesting sessions are, the level of Christian faith being taught, how Bible-centered the literature is, the need for a friendly spirit among the people, and so on.

The Church Ministers to People

Babies. Let's begin at the very beginning. When a baby is born in the congregation, the parents of that baby should be contacted. Putting that baby's name on the cradle roll or enrolling him or her in the nursery should be a big event. The cradle roll is important. There should be an ongoing plan, with someone in charge of enrolling new babies.

Children. Many parents bring their small children to Sunday school, but then there comes a time when that child begins to decide for himself whether or not he wants to come. This is when the Sunday school needs to show its strength. Does it have enough to attract young people?

Youth. We need to know that young people are not attracted to the church with a hot dog. Many have the mistaken idea that recreation is the way to attract young people. This is far from the truth. Recreation alone does not build youth interest. They get recreation many other places. They are looking for something serious and important. Genuine Bible study is more attractive to young people than many of us think. A lively youth music program gives the young people a chance to perform and is a blessing to the church when they do perform. When the young people realize that the church is serious business, they are much more apt to take it seriously. Recreation has been greatly overdone in our youth divisions.

Singles. There are other areas, such as single young adults. They are looking for friendships and especially for meanings in life. They are in the beginning of adult life, and many of them are floundering and afraid. The church has something to offer young people who wonder what their real purpose in life may be.

Couples. Young married couples especially need the church. The church can serve a good purpose in getting them involved. As they first begin their marriage they will be choosing life-styles, beginning careers, and perhaps making permanent friendships. Many church friends become the best friends a person ever makes!

As young couples begin rearing their children, they need the church more than ever. Many times this becomes the time when young adults become deeply serious about their own faith. They discover that they need to be able to speak clearly and honestly to their children, but also they realize that life has a new dimension and interest for them.

Somehow, the reality of God as Father, God as Creator, is more real to them. This age is one of the most productive in terms of commitment and creativity. The church, through its Sunday school, can reach, teach, and enable these young people.

Single Again. One of the most important groups in any community is what many churches call the single-again group. Divorce, for many persons, can be a more traumatic experience than death. Many of the loneliest persons in any city are single again. In the church in which we are now ministering, we organized what we call the Thirty-Nine Club. The only qualifications to belong to this club are to admit that you are thirty-nine, and are unmarried. It is amazing the friendships that have developed out of that club and the good it has done for a lot of people.

Middle and Older Adults. Middle and older adults also have their unique situations. Those with children face child-rearing problems, establishment of financial security for themselves and their children, and then later the empty-nest syndrome. Then there are singles who simply choose not to marry. There are those who are bereaved or lonely, those who are short-term residents of a community or city, professional persons, laborers, and those who are unemployed. There are the retired, the homebound, and so on. Experiences, concerns, viewpoints, and interests will vary.

Special Studies

There are enumerable places in which we can become strong where we are now weak. For example, do we have in our Sunday schools a group that seriously is interested in Bible study? Do we have a group that would like to spend its time discussing the application of the Christian faith to the society in which we live? The point is: Are we meeting the interests of the people in our Sunday schools?

There is a story that we ought to take seriously. A man built a factory to manufacture dog food. He built the finest, most modern factory that could possibly be built. Then he employed the best sales force that could be assembled. After six months, however, this company was practically bankrupt. He called in all of his people and explained that they had the finest factory and the best sales force, and yet they were failing. He asked what the trouble was. Someone spoke up and said, "The trouble is that the dogs do not like the food we are manufacturing."

We can have the finest building and the finest teachers and the finest officers, but if the people are not interested in what is being presented, we are certain to fail. Here is a point that we need to lay great emphasis upon: Are we presenting the teachings that minister to the needs of the people?

One of the great weaknesses of many churches is thinking that the Sunday school is only for children and youth. This could not be farther from the truth. The greatest opportunities for growth are in the adult divisions. The best way to grow in the adult divisions is to organize new classes. An adult class will grow to a certain size and then stop. No matter what we do, in most instances, the class will not get any bigger. It is easy to say we have no more room for new classes. We do have room. A class can meet in the choir loft on Sunday morning, or in the pastor's office, or in the church kitchen. Look over your church, and you can find a surprisingly large number of places where new classes could be started. They do not have to be large, spacious rooms. A class of a dozen can often be very effective and useful.

In the church where we serve, we have two morning services, with Sunday school between the two services. We discovered that about half the choir members did not go to Sunday school. Instead they would stay in the choir room, drink coffee, and talk. And so we started a Bible class in the choir room for the choir members. This session could not be lengthy. In fact it is limited to fifteen minutes, but in those fifteen minutes we read the Bible, we talk about the Christian life, and we have prayer. It has become a very effective class, and it has added a new spiritual dimension to the choir.

In the church we serve, there is another group which meets in the kitchen to drink coffee and talk every Sunday morning during Sunday school. It is easy to say that they should be in a class, but the truth is they are adults and they want to be in the kitchen, drinking coffee and talking. So we sent a teacher to them, and, standing there in the kitchen, the teacher talks to them about the Christian faith and about the Bible and has prayer. The entire formal part of the class probably lasts only ten minutes, but after it is over these people stay there and generally they talk among themselves about issues that were raised. It has really become an effective group in the church.

Many of us are very strong on grading our classes according to age. But in every Sunday school there ought to be at least one class that spans the entire age group. We can well imagine how a seventy-year-old person and a twenty-five-year-old could gain from each other in the same class. There ought to be a class that includes twenty-year-olds and seventy-year-olds and all in between. It can be one of the most effective classes in the entire Sunday school. Various age groups like to hear what the other age groups think and say. These are sometimes called intergenerational groupings.

Churches have discovered that families enjoy studying together and that they benefit greatly from such an experience. Children and youth, when allowed the freedom to explore and share with the same dignity accorded older people, have valuable contributions to make. Adults are moved to find their own faith answers. This type of class may open, for the first time, a communication channel between age groups.

Outreach

Of course it has long been said, but it needs to be constantly said, "Bring your children to Sunday school; don't send them." We keep repeating that Sunday school is not just for children and youth. It is also for adults of all ages.

We know of one church in a county-seat town where the pastor went to the leading men of the church. He said to each of these men, "Here is a list of four persons who live close to you. They are not in Sunday school, and they have no transportation. Would you be willing to pick them up and take them home each Sunday?" A surprisingly large number of the men agreed to do that. In this particular county-seat-town church, the Sunday school grew from an average attendance of one hundred fifty to four hundred.

Of course other churches have achieved marvelous results with a bus ministry. We send out buses and bring our children to public schools. Why not send a bus and bring persons to Sunday school?

Home Department

In looking at the weak places in your Sunday school, don't forget the home department. How many persons are there on the rolls of your church who, because of age or infirmities, are unable to come to church in person, but whose minds are alert, and they are still interested. Many of these persons feel completely left out. Why could not they be given literature to study and somebody in the church to visit with them and to talk with them and make them know they're a part of the Sunday school? They would not be present in person, but they would be present in spirit. Literature could be mailed to them, but it's better for it to be taken. There are persons in the Sunday school who would do that, and a delightful visit would result. The persons at home would be encouraged to study the material and would be considered a part of the Sunday school. Here is a very important thing: We would discover that many of these persons who think that they are not able to attend would find their interest growing to the point at which they would discover not only that they could but they would come to the church. Many members of the home department would become participating members of a class at the church on Sunday.

A study of the entire membership should be made, and those who are not able to attend should be listed. Then they should be enlisted in the home department, and this could be one of the most effective departments in the Sunday school.

It does no good for a group merely to sit down and talk about the weaknesses of their Sunday school. It does great good to sit down and identify the weaknesses and then talk about how those weaknesses can be strengthened and corrected.

For You to Do

We suggest that a committee make a careful listing of the age-group ministries the church is now engaged in. Consider every age group: children; youth; single adults; single again; young, middle, and older adults; homebound members; and all other groups. Then ask the question, "What can we do to strengthen each particular group?" In such a procedure it often happens that our greatest weakness becomes our greatest strength.

It is important to recognize who the persons are and what their needs and concerns may be. Everyone is not the same. There are all kinds of persons in varied situations. What reaches one may not necessarily reach the other. Think of support which the church needs to give.

1. Ask yourselves: Are new groupings needed? Would new settings be helpful? What other means of outreach could be used? Where will we find leadership? And how will we develop it?

2. After these questions are answered, write down a plan of action.

3. Spell out ways to implement it.

4. Assign responsibilities to persons.

5. Set a date which will be checkup time.

6. *Do* what you've planned to do.

5

The Campaign

We, in America, are familiar with campaigns. Almost every person who has ever been president of the United States or governor of a state or mayor of a city or held any other political office got there because of a definite campaign. All the charitable organizations in our nation which prosper do so because they put on campaigns. The same approach is needed in our Sunday school. The truth is that there should be a constant campaign all the time, but there also ought to be special times to do more than we are regularly doing.

In most churches, every year there is a campaign for pledges to the church budget. Without some kind of campaign, most churches would be financially embarrassed. We need several campaigns through the year to increase the effectiveness and attendance of our Sunday school. There need to be training and enrichment courses for our teachers and officers. There also need to be efforts to enlist those who have dropped out and to enlist those who have never enrolled.

Developing the Christian Education Ministry

In the June, 1977, issue of *The Church School,* a United Methodist publication, Warren J. Hartman, director of Church School Development in the United Methodist

Church, speaks of several churches and how they are developing their Christian Education ministry:

"In a church that is part of a larger parish the superintendent and children's teacher decided to concentrate on reaching more children for Christ and the church. In a few weeks' time the number of children enrolled had doubled. And they formed a choir that sings in the congregational worship service every week.

"In a large suburban church, the council on ministries assessed ways that members of the congregation were involved in the various activities of the church. The council discovered that a number of women were not involved in the church school because most of the adult classes were oriented toward married couples. To explore several possibilities four women were invited to meet with the director of Christian education. They decided to organize a class for women of all ages; in less than a year more than twenty women were enrolled. Furthermore, the average attendance in the total church school was increased by the exact number of persons who attended the new women's class.

"The pastor and education work area chairperson in a county-seat town church became concerned about the irregular attendance of a number of children and youth. They developed a plan for following up on absentees and visitors with a phone call or a personal visit. They now report that the average attendance in their church school has increased by 20 per cent.

"The director of Christian education in a downtown church discovered that most of the children in the church school had little contact with the young people or adults of the congregation other than their teachers. Furthermore, many of them came from homes where the parents were not involved in the church in any way.

"To help them all learn to know one another and share in meaningful experiences of worship and fellowship, they hold a modern adaptation of the old church school assembly one or two Sundays every month. Youth and adults are also encouraged to invite one or more of the children to accompany them to the congregational worship service that follows.

"In a rural church on the edge of a rapidly growing county-seat town a pastor and members of the council on ministries became concerned about the failure of their church to provide a satisfactory ministry to many of the young adults moving into their community. They planned several informal weekend events in which the pastor met with small groups of young adults to explore possibilities with them.

"As a result, a church school class was organized to meet on Sunday evenings with the pastor as teacher. Now several members of the group have become so deeply involved in the life of the church that they are not only attending the new young adult class but also teaching in the children's and youth divisions during the Sunday morning church school hour.

"Many of the children in an inner-city church day school come from homes without a father. They have few opportunities for positive experiences with men. The pastor and several of the teachers have invited some of the retired men of the congregation to work with the children on a frequent and regular basis. A number of supportive and growing relationships are developing as the men (some of whom are grandfathers with their own grandchildren living in other cities) play, study, and worship with the children in the day school. One eighty-four-year-old grandfather says this is the most rewarding experience the church has ever provided for him.

"In two circuit churches the pastor and leaders of the Sunday church school were struggling to develop a more effective Christian education program. After considering several options they decided that the church schools would benefit if both pastor and wife could work with them. They revised the church schedules so that they would have two-hour church school sessions in each church on two Sunday evenings each month. Attendance and interest picked up rapidly.

"A pastor discovered that more than seventy adults in the congregation were not involved in the educational program in any way. He mailed a letter to each, inviting them to meet with him during a Sunday church hour for coffee and an informal discussion.

"Approximately half of them came, and they agreed they would be interested in learning more about the Christian faith and its relationship to their daily lives. They further agreed that they would come to a new class, provided the pastor would agree to teach it. The class was formed with the understanding that it would be limited to adults who were not then enrolled in any other church school class.

"After a few months the average weekly attendance in the total church school had increased by nearly sixty persons. Not only has the new adult class grown, but other members of their families have also become more regular in their attendance.

"In a congregation with a large percentage of older persons, members of the church school became concerned about those who were now finding it difficult to participate as fully as they wanted to. They decided to invite every Sunday class to be responsible for several of the older members of the congregation each quarter.

"Now class members visit in the homes of the older persons, provide transportation as needed, phone them regularly, remember birthdays and anniversaries, and keep the pastor informed about any special needs that may arise. The pastor reports that a new spirit of Christian concern and love has developed in the entire congregation as a result. Increased interest and participation are especially

noticeable among the senior highs and young adults."
(Reprinted from *The Church School,* June 1977. Copyright
© 1977 by Graded Press.)

Many Sunday schools find it very effective to set a goal
for each class to strive toward. The goal should be large
enough to challenge the faith of the class, but not so large
as to make it impossible. Psychologically it is far better to
have a goal that can be reached and exceeded than to have
a goal which is too high and fall short. There is tremendous power in victory. When a class has achieved the victory, it becomes stronger than it ever was before.

Getting Support

In every church there are certain persons who are
natural salespersons. There is a story of a man who was
selling milking machines. He went to a farmer who had
one cow. He sold the farmer two milking machines and
took the cow in as part payment. He was truly a salesman.
Let's seek out these salespersons in our Sunday school and
add their talents to talents other persons have. Let's try to
fit the persons to the job. In every church there is this
group of persons who have ability to sell or motivate.
Their aid should be enlisted, and a definite attendance
campaign should be formulated.

An adequate campaign needs adequate financing. Here
is a place where a church can make an investment that will
pay rich dividends. Be sure to provide enough funds to
put on a campaign that will have an impact. The increased
attendance will more than pay for the expense.

Imagination should be used in beginning a campaign.
Definite plans should be made. The committee can think
up many things to do. Posters should be placed throughout the building. Committees should be formed. A timeta-
ble should be set. But, mainly, persons should be inspired
to believe that their Sunday school means business.

It needs to be greatly emphasized that support—enthusiastic support—must come from the pulpit. Unless the pastor gets excited, the church is not going to get excited.

In any campaign there should be a definite date, personal visitation, telephoning, letter writing, publicity, and, especially, prayer. All of it works together.

It is very important to have a progress report each Sunday during the campaign. Let the people know that you are succeeding. Nothing succeeds like success.

A main consideration in planning a campaign is the matter of holding the people, once the special climactic date of the campaign has passed. This planning of the follow-up is just as important as the buildup.

The main thing to be said is that any church can increase its enrollment and attendance if it is willing to work hard, but the price is not cheap. Hard work is hard work. By the same token a campaign must not be finished without including the follow-up program.

Leaders of the Sunday school should discuss the matter of whether or not they have ever really worked to increase attendance. It would be embarrassing in many Sunday schools to write down what they have done in a special way to make their Sunday school grow.

It can be done—in the name of the Lord Jesus Christ. Do it!

We need to remember that the Christian faith involves people. This illustrates what Christianity is all about. The cross that stands the tallest in the world is atop the Chicago Temple. There, in the loop of Chicago, stands this many-storied building. Above it is the cross. One day a repairman was up there doing some work on the cross. In the street below, hundreds of people were standing, looking up at the cross. Someone came by and remarked, "That cross has been there for years and years; and I have never seen people standing here, looking up at it. Why now?" An observer remarked, "There is a man on the cross now." Christian work is done by people in the name of the Man on the cross. And when we decide to make some sacrifices in His name and go to work for Him, we can increase the enrollment and attendance in our Sunday school far beyond our expectations. There are a lot of persons who will respond to a group of Sunday-school people who are serious.

For You to Do

Begin thinking about the possibilities of a campaign, and at some point plan one for your Sunday school.

6

If You Want More People, Make Your Sunday School Better

The one sure way to increase attendance and hold it is to make the Sunday school better. A campaign can increase attendance in the most inadequate Sunday school anywhere, but that increase will be lost very quickly unless the Sunday school itself measures up to expectations.

Establish the Real Purpose of Your Sunday School

A Sunday school which can define why it exists and what it is trying to accomplish is already one step ahead. At first this would seem like a simple thing to do, but that is not the case. Often a church will just drift aimlessly in its Christian Education ministry. A few good things will accidentally happen. Some of the teachers and leaders will have individual understanding which will motivate them. Use of whatever material is available will give some direction, be it right or wrong.

But imagine the power which can be released when a people as a group, in force, come to realize the profound significance of what it really means to be a teaching, nurturing, enabling body of Christ. They know the direction in which they want to move and are more able to set themselves in that direction.

How do you go about stating your objective?

Each church or denomination usually has an overall

statement of purpose for its educational ministry. It gives direction to all curriculum. The United Methodist Church's statement is as follows:

> The objective of the church as manifested through its educational ministry is that all persons be aware of and grow in their understanding of God, especially of his redeeming love as revealed in Jesus Christ, and that they respond in faith and love—to the end that they may know who they are and what their human situation means, increasingly identify themselves as sons of God and members of the Christian community, live in the spirit of God in every relationship, fulfill their common discipleship in the world, and abide in the Christian hope. (*Foundations of Christian Teaching in United Methodist Churches,* Copyright, 1960, 1969, General Board of Education of the United Methodist Church, p. 31.)

The American Baptists state their objective as follows:

> The objective of the church's educational ministry is that all persons be aware of God through his self-disclosure, especially his redeeming love as revealed in Jesus Christ, and, enabled by the Holy Spirit, respond in faith and love, that as new persons in Christ they may know who they are and what their human situation means, grow as sons of God rooted in the Christian community, live in obedience to the will of God in every relationship, fulfill their common vocation in the world, and abide in the Christian hope. (*Design for Teacher-Learning: Prospectus II*—1970–71, Valley Forge: American Baptist Board of Education and Publication, pp. 4, 5.)

The Missouri Synod Lutheran Church states its general objectives as follows:

General Goals. The following goals or objectives are taken from "A Guide to the Sunday School Standard." They speak of the general or overall goals of Christian teachers.

(a) To lead the pupil to a knowledge of the true God and to faith in Jesus Christ as his only Saviour and Lord;

(b) To lead the pupil to an appreciation of his status as a child of God and heir of eternal life;

(c) To lead the pupil into the truths of the Bible so that by a growing knowledge of the Word of God his Christian faith and character are built and developed;

(d) To lead the pupil into an understanding and appreciation of his status as a living member in the body of Christ and to train him to participate in the life and work of the church;

(e) To lead the pupil into an awareness of his Christian responsibilities toward home, community, and nation. (*Called To Teach Children: A Guide For Workers in the Church School,* Donald Hoeferkamp and Arnold C. Mueller, Concordia Publishing House, Saint Louis, Missouri, 1965, p. 21.)

One year, one local church stated its purpose and annual goals in the following way:

Purpose
Westminster United Methodist Church seeks to:
- Build a community united in its gratitude and commitment to God.
- Dedicate itself to a continuing growth in fellowship, faith, and discipleship.
- Proclaim and demonstrate to others this new life in Christ.

Goals

Westminster United Methodist Church will strive to:

- Increase involvement of its members and potential members in all of its program ministries and worship opportunities.
- Stress all aspects of evangelism.
- Evaluate, strengthen, develop, and coordinate its educational ministries to children, youth, adults, and families.
- Increase our sense of being a church family.
- Increase our opportunities for individual and group spiritual growth.
- Stress and increase opportunities for our members to be of service to others.

The important thing is for you to identify the purpose for *your* church and come to terms with it. Accept it and work for it to be accomplished. A workers' conference or an all-day retreat would be a good way for teachers, officers, and church staff to think through in the deepest way the direction in which they want to go and the purpose they have. We think it is good for a local church to use its denominational statement as a springboard but then make its own statement in the members' own words.

For many years the International Council of Religious Education had a profound statement which centered around eight key phrases: God, Jesus, Christlike character, a Christian social order, the Church, the Home, a Christian philosophy of life, the Bible. Decide what you want to happen in understanding and experience of these, and you will have a pretty basic statement.

An important thing is that teachers and leaders will know that their job is no superficial one. They will know that their very best will be needed and that it will be given for something worthwhile.

A Recruitment Plan for Securing Teachers and Leaders

In improving the Sunday school, let us keep emphasizing that the most important thing of all is the securing and training of an adequate supply of consecrated, tactful, and loving teachers.

Never say, "We do not have enough teachers within our church." The minute you say that it will be true. When you acknowledge defeat you are defeated. On the other hand when you say, "There are plenty of persons in our church capable of teaching in our Sunday school," you have already won the victory. That is true, and when you believe it, you will find them, persuade them, and use them. Any church has within its own fellowship all the teachers, officers, and leaders it needs to build a good Sunday school.

We know of a church to which a man gave an unusually large financial contribution. Someone asked him if he had ever given a contribution before. He replied that he had not. He was asked why he had not given a large contribution before. His answer was, "Nobody ever asked me before." The same principle applies to getting teachers. Here is the problem: In every church there are many persons whom nobody has ever asked.

Not only does every church have the talent it needs, but that talent must be recruited and trained. Let us follow Jesus' method for finding new workers. It is a method that never fails!

> But when he saw the multitudes, he was moved with compassion on them, because they fainted, and were scattered abroad, as sheep having no shepherd. Then saith he unto his disciples, The harvest truly is plenteous, but the labourers are few; Pray ye therefore the Lord of the harvest, that he will send forth labourers into his harvest.
>
> Matthew 9:36–38

Look carefully at Jesus' plan:

First, He made a survey. We read, ". . . when he saw the multitudes . . . ." He knew there were people available.

Second, He knew the people were not listed. He saw they were ". . . sheep having no shepherd." There are those who say there are no prospects for our Sunday school and church or for leaders, but they just have not looked around.

Third, He laid it upon the heart of His own workers that there are needs all around them. In our churches we talk about the need for missions, and many times we are thinking about some far-off land. Jesus saw the people around close by.

Fourth, He emphasized the need for more workers, ". . . but the labourers are few." Let no one in Sunday school say, "There is nothing for me to do."

Fifth, Jesus said "pray." When we begin praying for a larger and more effective Sunday school, something happens to us. There is an old story about a widow who lived in a rural community. She said to her neighbor that she needed some wood. Would he, that night, in his family prayers, pray that the Lord would send her a load of wood? He promised to do so. As that family prayed that night this man petitioned the Lord to send the woman a load of wood. The next morning he got up early and, as he went out, his wife asked where he was going. He said, "I am going to carry that woman some wood." Oftentimes we are the answer to our own prayers.

Sixth, Jesus did not try to do everything Himself. He had the good judgment to enlist the cooperation of other persons to help Him.

This plan will work in any Sunday school. Right here a caution needs to be lifted up. Oftentimes persons will volunteer for places for which they are not suited. However, a person should never be turned down. There is a place of service for every volunteer. It remains for the leadership of the Sunday school to know where those places are. It is wonderful to say to someone, "Thank you for volunteering for this particular place, but we need you more at this other place, and your service there will mean so much to the Sunday school."

Let us again emphasize the fact that Jesus said, "Pray ye therefore the Lord of the harvest, that he will send forth labourers into his harvest." We believe that God calls ministers. We further believe that God calls workers in every area of His kingdom. Every Sunday school should be undergirded with prayer. Let us always remember the words of the Lord, ". . . Not by might, nor by power, but by my spirit, sayeth the Lord of hosts" (Zechariah 4:6).

Part of a church's plan for its Sunday-school ministry should include the practical means of finding and enlisting persons to teach and lead. In some churches there is a committee appointed to attend to this. In others, special officers, such as the Sunday-school superintendent and the chairperson of Christian Education are charged with the responsibility. In very large churches the staff persons responsible for Christian Education will assist in the recruiting. Always the minister will be interested and involved.

Basic principles are:

1. *Know how many teachers, helping teachers, secretaries, and so forth you will need to recruit.* Children's classes and youth classes are completely staffed for them, with the youth usually electing their own officers. In the churches where we have worked, it has been the rule for general officers to be elected by the ruling body of the church, for teachers of adult classes to be commissioned to teach a particular group in concurrence with the desires of the group and the approval of the ruling body. Officers of adult classes are nominated and elected within each group. Make a list of the classes, how many teachers and leaders are required

for each, who of the present staff will continue, and, then, how many more are needed, and what they are needed to do. The moment a person says, "I really don't want to teach, but there's no one else to do it," relieve that person.

2. *Establish length of teaching term.* Often a person is willing to teach one year at a time, perhaps repeating over and over, but sometimes needing a year off. We do not believe a person should be coerced into teaching against his or her will. A happy thing to say is, "All the teachers in our church are teaching because they want to!" Say to prospects, "If you don't want to teach, we will not pressure you to do so. Perhaps you will want to teach later, or let us find something else which will interest you."

3. *Set some qualifications you want in a teacher.* One good way to secure this list is to get together some teachers and parents and ask them to name desirable qualifications. They will be more demanding of themselves than you. Such things as personal integrity, ability to communicate, evidence of openness and desire to grow and learn, willingness to follow objectives of the church, and so forth will probably be among the things which are listed. Write your qualifications down for a permanent record. Let your teachers-to-be know they are considered to be worthy of these qualifications and have been selected because of this.

4. *Establish a teacher-prospect list or a means of looking within your entire congregation for leadership.* One church we know uses a talent card to find out who plays the piano, who has had previous teaching experience, who would be willing to train to teach, and so forth.

Our church has a master file of all church members, listing helpful information about them. The recruiting committee may look here for needed talents.

We often go to the existing rolls of adult classes for emerging leadership. Adult classes should see themselves as preparing members for discipleship.

Another church keeps a family record card, showing

where each person, be it one or seven, is located. At special meetings such as a parents' meeting or a mid-week study group, the director of Christian Education and others responsible for recruiting are alert to notice persons who have the abilities to fit into a teaching responsibility. This observation is entered on the family card and, at the proper time, that person is invited to teach. Recruiters should constantly be on the alert for new leadership. A word of caution: Do screen carefully. Put the right person in the right place. Be sure they are willing to be part of the team.

Work out some plan for maintaining a teacher-prospect list.

5. *The invitation is most crucial!* If at all possible, go to the home of the person. The recruiters (who might be the superintendent of Study and the director of Christian Education or some other team) should call for an appointment, saying they have something important they want to talk over with the prospect, but waiting until they get there to actually give the invitation. They should take with them materials which are used in the class and explain how they are used. The recruiters should tell the prospect he or she has been selected, that the position calls for dedication, a lot of study, and much responsibility. They should outline how this position and class fits into the total scheme and share some of the joys which are present. Recruiters must have enthusiasm and zeal, and they must let it show.

Another excellent way to give the invitation is to set up an annual orientation class for prospective teachers. Go through your church membership files and select persons to invite to this. Let the class consist of sessions on the nature and mission of the church, the objective of the church through its educational ministry, the faith we teach, how to use the Bible in study, principles of teaching and learning, the I and thou of communication, and so on.

Ask the pastor or the director of Christian Education or a resource person from your denomination to teach. Use a weekend session, or a series of Sundays during the Sunday-school time. During these sessions, the new persons will be getting acquainted with each other; they will be learning valuable information; and leaders will be seeing strengths and needs of the new persons. At the end of the orientation, the new persons will be asked to teach or lead or help in a particular place, or they will be placed on the waiting list until needed.

Tell new persons you will support them with training and be readily available to them for help at all times.

Train and Nurture the Staff

In the training and development of workers and teachers, let us always remember there are two groups with whom we must work. The first group includes the ones who are already working. On-the-job or in-service training is extremely important. Just because a teacher is teaching does not mean he or she does not need additional training. A second group to train is the prospective workers. Even if you do not have a specific place for these workers at the moment, the very training makes them better members of a class and more effective workers in the Sunday school.

Let's examine some experiences which will be helpful in leadership development:

1. The orientation class is always a good place to begin. Even for persons who are already teaching, it is good to review from time to time.

2. Have a mid-week (or a time best suited to your church) series several times a year. Let these include studies on a selected book of the Bible, the art of communication, comparative religions, theology, history of the church, and so on. If your church is too small to set up a

series by itself, go in with one or more other churches. Secure the most capable leaders available. Enlist the aid of your pastor. This kind of training gives teachers great support! They teach with better understanding. Open the classes to other interested persons. (You'll find new people this way, too!)

3. Have regular workers' conferences. Depending on your situation, these may meet weekly, monthly, every other month, or quarterly. If this is the launching pad for other kinds of meetings and activities, such as calling or reviewing next Sunday's lesson, they will probably be weekly. If these are special occasions, quarterly is probably often enough. Remember this is not the only thing you're doing, and you don't want to drain people, but be helpful to them.

Some things to do at workers' conferences are: have an inspirational speaker and celebrate together the joy of being a teacher or leader; find out about community needs; learn about stages of development in people and the religious significance of these; share techniques for improving attendance in classes; do some how-to conferences. These may range from "How to Use Audiovisual Equipment," to "How to Plan a Unit and Session," or "How to Use Role Playing, Dramatization, Choral Speaking, and Creative Writing," and so forth. The list is endless and should be in keeping with your needs and goals. Involvement of the teacher or leader in the experience is always good. Experiencing, along with hearing, is important.

4. In one of the most successful Sunday schools which we have studied, we find that every Monday all the officers and teachers of the Sunday school meet together for lunch. The few who cannot make it for Monday lunch meet together for a snack supper on Wednesday evening. They tell us that coming together as workers, talking, planning, praying, thinking, studying as a team has done

more to increase the attendance, the spirit, and effectiveness of their Sunday school than anything they have ever tried. A church service can almost be a one-person affair. It can center around the preacher, but not so with the Sunday school; it is a team effort. In meeting together, gradually the weak links are discovered and either strengthened or replaced.

5. Workshops or seminars may be held for workers with a particular age group; these special meetings may concern specific things such as how to lecture, the use of curriculum resources, how to set up a room for a teaching or learning session, or the art of storytelling and its value. The list is endless.

6. Christian workers' schools—with certified leaders secured through your denomination headquarters—dealing with such things as how to teach kindergarten children, or how to teach youth or adults, can teach the characteristics of the age group, goals of learning for the age group, skills which will be helpful in communicating, using the resources, using the Bible in teaching, and so forth.

7. The laboratory school not only talks about the topics Christian workers' schools deal with, but provides experiences with the age group: Kindergarten teachers would actually plan a session, practice-teach, observe teaching, and be evaluated, as well as help to evaluate the teaching of others. A certified teacher who has prepared to do this is best. Contact your denomination headquarters. Remember, churches may group together for such enterprises.

8. Supervision by counseling teachers or other designated persons is a good training method.

9. Regular teacher meetings, to talk together about lesson materials, plan sessions, find out about additional resources, to discuss who the pupils are and what their needs are, are imperative. Secretaries, membership chairpersons, and other officers need regular meetings, too, to

check on record keeping, system of outreach, their program of evangelism, and so on. They need to understand the importance of their positions in sustaining a caring, nurturing ministry among their particular group, as well as leading them to care for others.

10. A recognition time for teachers and leaders is a nurturing act. It also teaches the church as a whole that Christian Education is a part of the church's ministry. We recommend an annual commissioning service in one of the regular worship services, with the teachers and leaders coming to the altar of the church for a time of dedication. Give the congregation an opportunity to pledge support through prayers and presence.

A climate for wanting to grow, as persons, in the Christian faith, for having a zeal for continuing education, for feeling the desire to reach out and share with others—all this takes time, but it comes. You plant the seed. God will give the growth.

For You to Do

1. Write your objective for your church. Involve many persons in doing it. Use your denominational statement as a springboard.

2. Formulate a plan for finding and securing teachers and leaders.

3. Design an ongoing plan for teacher/leadership development and nurture.

4. Implement your plans.

7

If You Want More People, Make Your Sunday School Better (Continued)

In the previous chapter, we talked about establishing an objective—the purpose—and the recruiting and training of teachers and leaders. These are vital concerns. A good Sunday school also gives attention to many other concerns.

Organization

Organization is just as important in the Sunday school as it is in a business, a corporation, a school system, a town, or city. First of all, the local church is responsible for its own organization. For this reason the pastor, as the executive officer, carries top responsibility, along with the guiding, official body of the church. Many churches also employ a staff person, or persons, to assist in its educational ministry. Almost always there is need for an education committee, or council, and, as size dictates, age-group and interest councils. All groups have to be responsible to the coordinating body and the overall governing body. Certain officers are elected by the church.

All the work of the Christian Education ministry is subject to the organizational rules and regulations. No one class or group, regardless of the setting, is an independent agency, a law unto itself.

Each church needs to choose some kind of competent, representative, governing group to determine policy and program and administer them. This group will, among other things, educate itself, do congregational analysis, see that the entire program is staffed, that there is no overlapping of program, and look for areas of neglect. It will help to determine constructive attitudes in the church and work for better cooperation of church and home—in short, all the things we talk about in this book and more.

Our concern is to build a better school and thus improve Sunday-school attendance. It all fits together. The successful Sunday school is organized. It runs like a well-oiled machine, seemingly effortlessly. But the truth is, it takes a lot of effort and a lot of persons doing their responsibility and knowing that what they do—be it handing out chalk, or filling out the secretarial report—is important. It all fits together.

Various denominations have different organization plans for their Sunday school. Get the organization chart of your denomination and follow it. Use the organization to get things done in an efficient, productive way.

There follow several areas which are done well if there is proper organization.

Record Keeping

A local church, through its classes, will show its interest in each person by having his or her name on the class roll. Accurate addresses and telephone numbers will be maintained. Each Sunday the class will know who is present and who is not. Designated persons will contact the absent members as an act of caring.

Reports on the numbers of persons present in departments and an overall total help to chart the well-being of the school. Too many absentees, a drop in average attendance, or a failure to grow when there is potential for growth, are all danger signals. This is the time to check the back door.

The system of record keeping is a matter of policy. Study neighboring churches. Read suggestions from your own denomination. Be innovative in your own right.

Record keeping is important. We all like to count for something; and to count for something, we need to be counted. Every class ought to make a habit of counting those present. The very act of being counted stimulates the desire to be present and to get others to come, too. Of course, after the counting must come the follow-up. We keep emphasizing follow up. Let us not be weary. Let us continually follow up. Someone who is sick needs to be reminded that somebody else cares. Someone who is losing interest needs to be reminded that somebody is interested in him or her. Interest begets interest. It is an easy thing to take a class roll and mark off those who have not been present over a certain number of Sundays. It is a much harder, but better, thing to get in touch with those persons and win them back. Making persons feel that they are wanted and loved goes a long way in keeping the attendance up; persons need to be told that they are missed. This takes time and effort, but unless a Sunday school is willing to pay the price, it is not going to reap the reward.

Greeters

Someone, or a group of people, depending on your needs, should be designated to be present each Sunday, near the entry or entries. These persons should greet the Sunday-school attenders as they arrive and welcome them with a handshake, a smile, and, "Glad to see you!"

Visitors should be shown to an information desk, where greeters will inform them of available classes. Fill out a visitor's form (for the records, and follow-up) on them. Have designated persons on standby to escort them to classes and introduce them to greeters in the classrooms.

This simple, easy-to-do service will create a wonderful

spirit in your church. It may make the difference in your keeping or losing a newcomer. Be prepared. Be gracious. Be friendly.

Equipment and Environment

Another way of improving Sunday school is improving the equipment and environment. Some churches can afford to build the buildings they need and buy all the equipment they can use. On the other hand, in other churches there are men and women with skills. Some are carpenters, others are electricians, others can paint, others can sew. Get those people together certain nights of the week and on Saturday. Repaint the furniture. Put up attractive new curtains. Change the color of the walls. Build tables and toys and chalkboards. Amazing things can be done with some willing hands and very little money.

In cleaning and refurbishing, do not leave out the children and young people. They like to be included. Let six- and seven- and eight-year-old children feel that they helped to do something to make their church better and prettier. They take great pride and joy in feeling that they helped.

Some Sunday schools feel they lack money. We know of one church which invited the parents of the children's division to visit the rooms one particular Sunday morning. As they looked around, one of the teachers diplomatically said, "Would you parents like to pass the hat this morning to help us get the money to make these rooms prettier for your children?" It is amazing what parents will do when their own children are involved. Needless to say, the money was raised, and everybody lived happily thereafter. They could have had a bake sale or a bazaar, or a country carnival.

Proper ventilation and heating or cooling should be provided.

Maybe you do not have the building you would like, but be sure the one you have is as clean and as attractive as you can make it.

Space

In a growing Sunday school, from time to time, classes need to be moved from one room to another. This can be a very delicate problem. Classes become attached to certain rooms. But when you have a class with forty in attendance meeting in a room designed for thirty and another class with an average attendance of thirty meeting in a room designed for forty-five, it is obvious that a change needs to be made. But it needs to be made very diplomatically and not too hastily. Cooperation of everybody concerned must be lovingly sought.

It is a wise thing for the governing body to remind all concerned that spaces are studied periodically and that no one room belongs to any certain class or group.

Children need more square footage than adults, because they move about, in interest centers, during their Sunday school. They need space. The crib room and other nursery rooms need to be especially convenient. Young families need the church. The church needs young families and is concerned about them.

Library–Resource Center

Every church should have a library or resource center. A volunteer who will become informed about procedures and materials and a library or resource committee should be appointed to oversee this important support system.

Carefully selected books, maps, audiovisuals, charts, pictures, and so on should be catalogued and readied for check out. Teaching pictures should be mounted on cardboard and identified on the back. From time to time there should be a session of sharing for the teachers. New books should be shown, and teachers need to know that supplementary material is available for them.

Some churches use the satellite system, in which filmstrips, slides, maps, globes, and pictures are made available from one center, equipment and supplies from another center, books and magazines in another center, with reading tables and comfortable chairs available.

The very small church may have only a few shelves in a corner. It doesn't take much space to add a small bookcase. An enterprising, resourceful person might keep the library in his or her home; but, each time the study emphasis changes, bring a traveling library to the teachers. A good, sturdy box to hold the books can be decorated and handholds made on each end.

One word of caution: Do not fill up your library shelves with books that nobody is ever going to use, like outdated books from someone's home. It is much better to have a few current books that are useable and meaningful. Your denominational board of education will regularly supply you with a list of books that are helpful and meaningful in supplementing your teaching program. Pay careful attention to that list of books. Let it be known in the church that books can be given to the library as memorials or as a way of showing appreciation to someone. It is surprising how many will be received in this way. However, let it be understood that the memorials should be given in the form of money, and the library committee will select the books. Buy the books recommended by your denominational board. Usually, they will give you a library discount. One of the worst things that can happen in any church is to get books in the library which are contrary to the doctrines and practices and teachings of that particular church.

Curriculum Resources

The greatest care should be exercised in selecting the curriculum resources. A good system is to have a literature secretary. The literature secretary is in charge of the order blank which comes from the denominational headquarters. (The pastor or other staff person will submit the name on request.) At the proper time, department heads will submit their literature needs to the literature secretary, who will in turn order, receive the materials, count and check, divide as needed for classes, deliver to proper rooms, and submit the invoice to the church office for payment. Record keeping comes in very handy here, as departments have to determine well in advance how much material to order.

Basic curriculum resources will be listed for a particular study. The literature secretary works closely with responsible staff persons, with department heads, directly with teachers at times, and with the librarian or resource-center chairperson. In a small church, the same person might be literature secretary and librarian.

Your Sunday school will be better if you have *good* resources to use.

Reaching Out

Let the people know about your Sunday school. Publicize your Sunday school, talk about it, inform people through the church paper and Sunday bulletin. Create a climate of awareness and support. The pastor can do more than any other person to set the mood of the church toward Sunday school.

Work with sister churches, other denominations, and your church support systems beyond the local level. Great help is available through these avenues. You also grow as you give and share.

The Great Commission in Action

So we want to increase our attendance in Sunday school. We want our school to be a better one. In truth, increasing attendance in the Sunday school is not something for us to decide. Literally it is the command of God. Ever so often we need to read again Matthew 28:19, 20:

> Go ye therefore, and teach all nations, baptizing them in the name of the Father, and of the Son, and of the Holy Ghost: Teaching them to observe all things whatsoever I have commanded you: and, lo, I am with you alway, even unto the end of the world. Amen.

As we read the Great Commission we note that it begins with the word *go.* Nowhere in the Bible does Jesus command persons to come to the church, but over and over He commands Christians to go out and find others and bring them to the church. Before we emphasize *come,* we need to emphasize *go.* Let those of us who are in the Sunday school go; then there will be many others who will come.

Notice also in the Great Commission that our Lord said *teach.* That is the business of the Sunday school. It is not a preaching service. Most of the Sunday-school classes are not held in the sanctuary. It is a time of teaching in a classroom. Read the four Gospels, and you find that Jesus spent a lot more time teaching than He did preaching. Once a man said to Jesus, ". . . we know that thou art a teacher come from God . . ." (John 3:2). To that man Jesus spoke the greatest statement that has ever been spoken on earth: "For God so loved the world, that he gave his only begotten Son, that whosoever believeth in him should not perish, but have everlasting life" (John 3:16). Let us always remember that He spoke those matchless words as a teacher.

There is a lovely story about a Chinese man who became a Christian. His name was Lo. A missionary gave him a Bible. One day Lo rushed to the missionary and said, "My name is in the Bible." He turned to the Great Commission, where it says, ". . . Lo, I am with you alway" (Matthew

28:20). He believed the Lord was actually speaking to him, and you know we believe the same thing. We believe that when a person is seeking to do God's work He will keep His promise and be with that person, no matter what happens. We must reemphasize the fact that we are commanded by God to go and to teach, but we are also promised that He will be with us always, no matter what happens.

Improving the organization, training the teaching staff, obtaining better literature, providing a more adequate library, improving the building and equipment—all these are important. But in really improving the Sunday school the most important thing is the presence of God, through Christ, in the lives of those of us who are working for Him. If we possess God, somehow we'll find a way to share Him.

For You to Do

1. Evaluate your organization plan.

2. Be sure your church is properly organized to carry out its Christian Education ministry.

3. Check each subhead, and any other categories you think of, for efficiency in your Sunday school. Set up those which you do not already have.

8

Evangelism in the Sunday School

If we were to ask every member of our Sunday school the question "what is the purpose of the Sunday school?" we would get many answers, and all of them would be good. We would get such answers as: to teach the Bible, to build fellowship among the church members, to provide recreational opportunities; and these and other reasons for the Sunday school justify its existence. But the supreme reason for the Sunday school is to win persons to Jesus Christ as their Saviour, Lord, and Friend. The Sunday school is the chief evangelistic agency of the local church. Evangelism is not the only business of the church, but it is the main business of the church. When we cease to become evangelistic, then our reason for existence is over.

A familiar passage of the Bible might be paraphrased to read this way: "There was a church which grew to large numbers, and the people said to themselves, 'What should we do, for we have no room for our children or for those who wish to worship with us? This we will do. We will build greater buildings, so that our children can receive a religious education and people who have never known Christ can be invited into our fellowship.' And we will say to our souls, 'Souls, ye have a great church which will be adequate for many years. Take thine ease.' " But God said to them, 'Ye fools this night thy souls will be required to thee' "

(Luke 12:16–20). So it is with any church when it becomes satisfied. The work of the church will never be finished until the last person on this earth is won to Jesus Christ.

School for Sinners

There are those who contend that the church is a community of saved people. There are others who disagree with that view, but surely there is no argument when we say that the Sunday school is a school for sinners. The Sunday school is a place in which many may become Christians.

Not very long ago, a man said to one of the ministers of the church where we work, "Will you tell me how to be a Christian?" The business of the Sunday school is to answer that question to every person who comes.

Persons need to have religious knowledge. A powerful tool for evangelism is the Bible. It speaks directly to persons today, even as it did yesterday. Bible study is exciting and alive. Churches everywhere are experiencing more interest in the study of the Scriptures than ever before. Many classes set up additional through-the-week studies to add to their Sunday-school time. We need to keep our eyes open to this evangelistic opportunity. Make your Sunday-school time the hub of all that happens.

Beliefs

The beliefs of persons, as well as their philosophies of life, make a difference in their actions. The Christian faith is an active force, and the church needs to help each person have an opportunity to grow in personal faith. What does one believe about God? about Jesus? about human nature? about prayer? and so on. Christians have many different understandings of the great themes, but a diligent search together can be an uplifting spiritual experience—a powerful way to enable persons to respond to God's seeking love, to His demands upon their lives.

Many times in our Sunday school we use words and phrases that sound good, but which do not mean a lot. For example, some might say, "You need to come to Jesus." That is true, but a lot of people would not know how to do that. In the great old theological statement "you need to be washed in the blood," there is certainly truth, but we also need to be able to explain what that means. One of our weaknesses in the Sunday school is using phrases and words that are not understood. We need to realize the needs of small children and understand how they conceptualize words. Sometimes we are like the preacher who could speak the word *Mesopotamia* in such a beautiful way that it made people cry. But it didn't do them any good; it just made them cry.

Find Them

Turn to the fifteenth chapter of Saint Luke's Gospel and read that beautiful story which Jesus told about the shepherd and the sheep. It begins, "What man of you, having an hundred sheep, if he lose one of them . . ." (Luke 15:4). There you have represented the shepherdless. That lost sheep was not a bad sheep. It probably was as good as the other sheep, but it was out eating grass, and the grass was good, and it gave all of its attention to the grass and forgot to look up and keep the shepherd in sight. After a while it became dark, and this sheep was lost. In our communities there are vast numbers of people who are not angry with God, who are not bad people, who do not want the church destroyed, but who get interested in other things and gradually reach the point where they have left God out of their lives.

It is not our business to condemn the lost. It is our business to go out and find them. There is a story about a church in a small town. The church caught on fire one night. All the people of the town came to the fire. The preacher went around shaking hands with the people, and he came to one man and said, "I am glad to see you. This is the first time I have ever seen you at church." The man replied, "Preacher, this is the first time your church has ever caught on fire."

The business of the church is to teach the Gospel of Jesus Christ. Here we need to emphasize the fact that the word *Gospel* literally means "good news." Many of us believe that the greatest Christian utterance, other than the words of our Lord, is 1 Corinthians 15:1. There Paul begins with the words, ". . . I declare unto you the gospel. . . ." Many times we can tell the truth and yet not be teaching or preaching the Gospel. We can say, for example, that diphtheria is a bad disease. That is true, but it is not good news. If we say, however, that there is a vaccine which can prevent diphtheria or cure diphtheria, that is the good news.

We can say that people are sinners and that the world is bad. And we would be telling the truth, but that is not the good news; it is not the Gospel. When we say that here is One who can save a person from sin, who can make a bad world good, that is the good news; and that is the Gospel. The Sunday school that wins is the one which has a positive message of hope and inspiration.

Born Again

Evangelism means bringing persons into a personal relationship with Jesus Christ. Many of us have believed that one should grow up believing himself or herself to be a Christian and never knowing anything else. Of course we all know that Jesus said, "Ye must be born again." Becoming a Christian is by the method of the new birth, but many who have grown up in the loving, tender nurture of a Christian Sunday school can experience that new birth in such a gentle way that it is not the traumatic experience which Saint Paul had.

Someone said, "We do not have revivals like we used to have." Some may remember revivals in which unusually emotional arousals would pressure persons into the kingdom. The Sunday school seeks to make that type of evangelism unnecessary. No one can make the personal acceptance or commitment to Christ for another person, but through the Sunday school we can make that commitment and acceptance more attractive, more intelligent, more positive, and more complete.

Christian Nurture

Furthermore, the Sunday school is concerned with Christian nurture. We know that the beginning of the Christian life is the new birth. We also know that when a baby is born it needs a lot of loving, a lot of attention, a lot of training. True evangelism works patiently and lovingly to keep the Christian experience a growing experience in the life of the person.

There is a story of a little boy who came crying to his mother one night, saying that he had fallen out of his bed. The mother asked why he fell out of his bed, and his reply was, "I went to sleep too close to where I got in."

It is the business of the Sunday school to keep the Christians from ever going to sleep spiritually. In every sense the Sunday school is a school of Christ. Caring people within a church, and especially within a Sunday-school group, give needed support to each other.

One of the mistakes often made in churches is deciding that children should make their commitment and become formal members of the church at a particular age. Here we must be very careful. One of the important functions of some churches is the membership training class or confirmation class. It is customary that out of this class the children are then formally brought into the membership of the church. Let us not be too rigid at this point. Not all children are alike. Some mature earlier than others. Some make a response to Christ at a different age than the one we normally set.

A true story comes to mind at this point. A certain little boy came to his father and said that he wanted to be received into the membership of the church. This was in February. The father called the pastor and conveyed the desire of his son. The pastor replied that they would have their membership class during the six Sundays leading up to Palm Sunday and that all the children would be received into the membership of the church on Palm Sunday. But the father insisted that his son wanted to join next Sunday. The pastor would not give in. He said, "Your son must wait until we have the membership class, and he can join the church with the other children." Tragically, the following week that little boy fell into a pool and was drowned. That father has since said, "I will never go back to a church which refused my child."

We feel that persons should be allowed and encouraged to make the Christian decision at the dictates of their own hearts. However, it is important that every person in the Sunday school, not only children, but young people and adults as well, from time to time be given definite and specific membership training. Training for responsible discipleship adds joy and depth to a person's lifelong participation in the church.

We recognize the need for children to be taught about church membership, but this needs to be a continuing process. Every year there ought to be certain periods set aside in every class for the teaching of the meaning of Christian discipleship and church membership. In churches where infant baptism is practiced, the confirmation class is in order. The persons accept their baptism for themselves and make a commitment to Christ. The church confirms them in this. We emphasize that the Sunday school never ceases to be interested in continued Christian nurture.

The Teacher as Evangelist

A teacher could take the following steps toward evangelism:

1. Find out whether or not every member of the class is a committed Christian. We must constantly emphasize the fact that being a Christian comes as a result of a personal decision.

2. The teacher of each class must have a special prayer list of those who have not knowingly accepted Christ. Praying for one by name transmits power.

3. In the spirit of prayer, private conversation should be sought. It is right and proper to speak to the class about Christian decision. It is also proper to speak privately and personally to seeking persons—always in the spirit of love.

4. When one makes the Christian decision, the teacher should stand by that person, helping them to, in the words of Saint Peter, ". . . grow in grace, and in the knowledge of our Lord and Saviour, Jesus Christ. . ." (2 Peter 3:18).

One of the best and most effective teachers' meetings which can be held is an evening spent letting each teacher tell of his or her decision for Christ, explaining the circumstances that led to it, and what influences were the strongest. Such a meeting not only inspires, it also teaches, and gives us insights into how to bring others into that wonderful experience with Christ. Let us constantly ask ourselves what our church is doing to bring continued growth in Christian life.

For You to Do

At a meeting, let the teachers and leaders of the Sunday school discuss such questions as:

1. What is our church's method in securing decisions for Christ in church membership?

2. Do we have an adequate membership training class?

3. Throughout our Sunday school, do we give enough attention to the question of what it means to be a Christian?

4. What does church membership mean?

9

The Sunday School Is a Part of the Church

Oftentimes we hear someone refer to the Sunday school as something apart from the ministry of the church. This is extremely erroneous. The Sunday school *is* a part of the church; the Sunday school is the church at work in Christian Education. It is just as much a part of the church as the worship in the sanctuary or pastoral care or any other mission of the church. The Christian church is persons who believe in God through Jesus Christ. They gather together in the church building to worship, to study, to fellowship, and to care. They go out to share, to witness, and to live their Christianity wherever they are.

Let it also be emphasized that often a word spoken quietly by some dedicated teacher to a small group in a Sunday-school class may be far more fruitful than a sermon preached that Sunday, in a sanctuary, to the entire congregation. The loving care displayed by persons within a class often reveals the love of God in a special way. The church and the Sunday school are part and parcel of the same ministry. Let there be no gulf fixed between the two.

There are several dangers we must guard against. One is that sometimes a Sunday-school class will become a church within the church. The teacher becomes a substitute for the preacher, as far as the members of that class are con-

82

cerned. It has its own budget and its own activities. Sometimes a class is not a part of the whole.

Another problem is that some members of the Sunday school may feel the Sunday-school class is enough. They feel that there is no reason to worship in the church service. When that happens, the Sunday school has failed. The two must go together: teaching and fellowship in the class and worship in the sanctuary. The church is far greater than any of its parts, including any Sunday-school class, or even the entire Sunday school.

Bridging the Gap

Sunday-school classes should develop in their members a general feeling that they also belong in the church service. Conversely, from the pulpit, the pastor of the church should develop in the worshipers the understanding that there is a place for each one of them in the Sunday school.

There are many ways of bridging the gap between the Sunday school and the church service. One way is through music. Multiple choirs, involving various ages and providing opportunities to participate in the worship service, can be very helpful. Some churches have a short sermonette for young children during the church service. At times classes are encouraged to attend church as a group and are so recognized. Teachers and officers are invited to be consecrated on a particular Sunday. Enterprising church staff and church-school lay leaders can come up with many ideas to make the Sunday school and the church one united effort for the Lord.

This is not the place to discuss the difference between teaching and preaching. The truth of the matter is that we are not sure that we know the difference between the two. Good teaching is preaching, and good preaching is teaching. The Sunday school and the church service provide different settings and different atmospheres which really accomplish the same purpose. Having the two doubles our chances of bringing our people into a fuller and more complete relationship and understanding of Jesus Christ. One of the goals in every church is not only to have Christians, but to have intelligent Christians. The Sunday school and church working together is the best way to achieve that end.

It is well for a representative group of the church worship service and Sunday school to plan a meeting sometime and talk together about the relationship of the two. The question might be asked, "How many Sunday-school persons also attend church services?" Also, cards might be passed out and a survey taken in the church service seeking to know how many churchgoers are in the Sunday school. With that knowledge, appropriate actions can be taken.

We emphasize the fact that no class should be a little congregation. Every class must be a part of the total church. There is a story which confirms this point. A large scaffold had been erected about the entrance of a church building. There were several workmen on the scaffold. A stranger stopped and asked, "What are you doing to this church?" One of the workmen replied, "Well, you see, they had some front doors here which were very heavy, and we are putting up some which are easier to operate." Then, with a knowing look, the stranger said, "No church has a right to put up doors that little children cannot open."

A similar story is the one about an artist who was at work at his easel, which was set up in front of a beautiful church. Some children passed by and watched him as he carefully worked at putting the church on the canvas. Finally one of the children spoke up and said, "Mister, would you mind putting us in the picture?"

It is the business of the church to make it easy for the

members of the Sunday school to be a part of the whole church—to be in the total picture.

For You to Do

In a church meeting, determine how your church might give joint support for both the Sunday school and the worship services.

10

More Than One Hour on Sunday

We have stated that some persons feel that it is a waste to build a room that will only be used for one hour a week. Our reply is: That hour is the most important hour of the week. Having said that, we come to the question of using that room or that building for extending that Sunday school beyond just that one hour. There are 168 hours in a week, and one hour per week is not adequate for the religious training of Christians, whether they be children, youth, or adults. Honest efforts must be made to increase the program of a church, if it is to accomplish its highest purposes.

A successful Sunday ministry for young children is the use of a two-hour expanded session. This means that for two whole hours nursery, kindergarten, and even first and second graders have the benefit of a learning, nurturing experience, under the leadership of trained teachers and workers. The children are relaxed, enjoy the participation, and eagerly look forward to it each Sunday. Parents or responsible persons who bring the child are free to attend an hour of worship and an hour of Sunday school. In the church where we work, this program has been used successfully for many years. It did away with the need for child care during worship service and greatly enhanced the teaching ministry for children.

Expand Beyond Sunday

One of the most fruitful activities of a church is the Vacation Church School or Vacation Bible School. In this experience of one, two, or three weeks, children and youth can be given concentrated instruction which it is not possible to provide on Sundays. Every denomination has careful and detailed plans for such a school. The very best leaders should be enlisted. They should be trained. The literature the denomination provides should be used to its fullest potential. Most important, every child and youth should be enrolled.

In a well-planned Vacation School, as much instruction can be given in this short time as can be given the remainder of the year in the Sunday sessions. It does not establish the weekly pattern of being present, but it is through this Vacation School that many new persons may be attracted to the total program.

There are other opportunities for children and youth ministry at the church house in weekday instructions. In many communities the Sunday school can work with the public school, providing instruction in the early morning before classes begin or in the afternoon after the public school has dismissed. This is easier to do in a small town than in a large city, but in many instances it has been done most successfully.

Day nurseries and day kindergartens are parts of the ministry of many churches. Christian teachers, usually extremely well trained and equipped to understand the children, study the faith and how it may be shared with young children through play experiences, storytelling, reading, and real-life experiences from day to day. Leaders and teachers in these schools do a great deal to give youngsters a good feeling about themselves, to free them to be creative, as God intended, and to be receptive for His seeking love.

Working mothers or fathers find day care in a Christian environment to be a precious help. A Mother's Day Out Program, where the mother may leave her child or children for a few hours, helps the child to be more independent and gives the mother some free time for herself. A church can easily provide this at low cost or provide the facilities and allow mothers to form a co-op. Care should be taken that nurturing procedure is used anytime the child is in the church building. To the child, church is church. Either love for it, or dislike for it can develop on Tuesday or Thursday and aid or destroy Sunday. This goes for all mid-week child care as well.

Throughout the year, special teaching situations can be developed, embracing various age groups, and at times all age groups. We think of such things as music-appreciation week, special weeknight study groups, religious-art studies, special dramas and pageants, Bible-study seminars, personal-growth seminars, marriage-enrichment groups.

We have alluded to special groups within the church community. Their number is almost unlimited. Many churches have art classes, sewing classes, book reviews, senior-citizen days, single-young-adult nights, and so on. Imagination and leadership can make a church both a seven-day church and a seven-night church.

First Things First

Never lose sight of what is important. Two illustrations come to mind:

A circus consists of the main tent and various sideshows. It is a tragedy for one to go to the circus and spend all the time in the sideshows and miss the main tent. Never forget that the main tent of the church is what happens on Sunday. All of the other activities are secondary. However, the weekday activities can be very supportive in gaining interest of other persons and maintaining interest of ones within the church.

In a very populous, affluent area, a beautiful shopping center was built. However, it later went bankrupt. Someone who knew the facts explained that the shopping center was built completely of "cluster" stores. There was no main store in the shopping center. This person went on to explain that a successful shopping center must have a main store. Then the cluster stores can be built around it. So it is with the church. Sunday is the main store. The activities of the week are the cluster stores. Let us never forget that when the main store closes, pretty soon the cluster stores will be gone, too.

For You to Do

A very fruitful activity in any Sunday school would be to pass out slips of paper asking persons of all ages to write their own particular interests and some activities in which they would enjoy participating. It might be very surprising how you would immediately have groups that fit into the same activities, and these could be started with most fruitful results.

11

The Sunday School and the Family

A Christian family, recognizing themselves to be a part of God's family, has a special nurturing ability, a special affirming quality, because of who its members are.

The home should be the primary teacher of religion. Home and church must work together in Christian nurture, because each has much to offer. The Sunday school should supplement and reinforce the Christian atmosphere of the home. Take-home materials will give parents and teachers an opportunity to share in teaching.

In our complex society today there are many types of families: the traditional (first marriage, mother and father and children at home), regrouped (remarriage, new spouses, children from previous marriages), broken (divorced or separated), multigenerational (more than one generation in the same house), and one parent and child or children. This complicates our task and makes it even more vital that we be steadfast to our purposes.

Encouraging Families

The Sunday school has a responsibility to the family, even as it does to the single adult. When a family, as a family, becomes active in the church, its members find a source of strength for themselves; they become more responsible people. Their life-style reflects their beliefs.

Parents are usually very quick to assume teaching and leading roles in the school of the church. Skills and insights they learn in leadership training are often very helpful in the home.

We recall how one young mother and father began a study on listening—really listening with full attention and with all their senses. They became aware that they had not been really listening to their six-year-old. It probably eventually made the difference between a turned-off teen and a communicating one.

The Sunday school has long brought the family to the church and then divided it into age groups, sometimes even separating male and female. Today a challenging concept, that of allowing families to study in family groups, is being tried by some churches. Some ministries can be achieved better through family groupings than any other way.

Programs which may be offered for families may be set during National Family Week, special family nights, family camps, or retreats. Family-life ministry could include preparation-for-marriage courses, nursery home roll and visitation, preparation-for-parenthood courses, and so on, as needs are established.

A Sunday-school class could be established for young parents or parents of teenagers. We know of one such group. They have studied developmental stages of children, the family in a changing world, how to communicate, the importance of a good beginning, and are presently deeply involved in a Bible study, seeking to firm up their beliefs, having realized that you have to know what you yourself believe before you can begin to share it with your child.

Families should be encouraged to participate in the

great religious seasons of the church. Tradition gives a person security. The great traditions of linking home celebrations with church celebrations tie the home and church together profoundly. Most familiar of these, perhaps, is Christmas, when we celebrate the birth of our Lord.

One church uses the whole season of Advent (four Sundays and related days prior to Christmas Day) to promote family worship services. A workshop showing families how to make Advent wreaths and work up simple services is held prior to the season. Simultaneously, each class in the Sunday school uses the Advent wreath for a brief worship time on Sunday morning. For many families, this has been the beginning of Bible reading and praying together.

Children cannot come to Sunday school unless they are brought. Youth, most often, will not establish the habit of coming, unless parents set the example. It is imperative that the decision makers of a household be cultivated.

The church and the home need to work together.

For You to Do

Think of ways your church can minister to its families.

1. Survey your church membership and your community or area. Find the families who are not in Sunday school. Invite them to a family-night dinner, and introduce them to representative class members who are present.

2. Or start a new class for them.

3. Activate the nursery home department.

4. Begin a class for parents of young children or one for parents of teenagers.

5. Plan a stock-the-food-bank drive, involving families. Lead parents to help their children to consider food as God's gift and to become aware that there are people in the world who are starving. Set aside one Sunday for canned goods to be brought to class for the food bank. Let

the children understand it will help feed a hungry person. Eat bread and water that day.

6. Prepare home-study packets including pictures, tapes, and suggestions for study. Encourage families to use these when they cannot be in class or when on vacation.

7. Ask families with children to adopt a "grandparent" from the congregation or community, invite that person to eat with them, attend Sunday school and worship with them, and so forth.

Continue thinking and planning. There are many ways to enrich lives through family ministry.

12

Permanent Values From the Sunday School

The main purpose of the Sunday school is to enable persons to become Christians, to nurture them, and to train them. In order to do these things, there are certain basic principles, practices, and truths which must be kept in mind. Let us list some of the basics of an adequate Sunday school.

The Bible

Learning the existence of the Bible is one of the basics of the Sunday school. Of course everybody knows there is a book called the Bible, but the fact is that vast numbers of persons have no knowledge of what the Bible is about and what it might mean to them and their society.

The Bible is the textbook of the Sunday school. There is some validity in the criticism which we have heard in recent years that the Sunday school does not teach enough of the Bible. In fact, Bible school might be a better name for the Sunday school. The ignorance of many church people about the Bible is really appalling. Recently, in one church an active member asked one of the teachers how to find certain books in the Bible. The teacher showed the person the index in the front of the Bible; the person was delighted and surprised. That person did not know such an index even existed. Persons need help in knowing how to use a concordance, a commentary, parallel Bibles, and so on. And there are those who probably need help in finding the books of the Bible.

For many persons the Bible is a closed book. It is closed because of lack of use. How many Christians ever read the Bible on their own initiative? They should be encouraged to read and study it. This is one of the purposes of the Sunday school. To many persons the Bible is closed because they feel that they cannot understand it. To them it is one great, mysterious puzzle. The Sunday school needs to teach persons how to read the Bible, something of its background and authorship, something of the day in which it was written, and the purpose of the Bible. There is very little opportunity to give much background study of the Bible from the pulpit. The Sunday school must do this very important work. We must teach our people to read the Bible uncritically, with imagination, and with their hearts as well as their minds. Let us never forget that the main literature of the Sunday school is the Word of God: the Bible.

Belief in God

The Sunday school needs to undergird persons' beliefs in God. One who was not a professing believer in God would hardly go to Sunday school. However, many persons are what we call practical atheists. We believe in the existence of God, but multitudes of people do not believe that God really makes any difference in their lives and in their world. The Bible never felt the necessity for proving the existence of God. The purpose of the Bible is to reveal God; it is a progressive revelation of God. There are those who say that they can find God in nature, in the lives of other people, in history, and in other places. But were it not for the knowledge of God that we have in the Bible, we would not see Him in these other ways.

We need to teach in our Sunday schools that God made the laws by which this world operates and that He made the laws by which people live. There is a feeling among many people that they can live as they please, but God said there are some things we cannot do. There is such a thing as breaking the law of God, being separated from God, and that is called sin.

One of the greatest problems in our world today is loneliness. More and more people are living in big cities. Cities become indifferent. People get lost in a city. We need to teach people that there is a God who knows them, who loves them, and who understands them.

The Christian Way of Life

The Sunday school teaches the Christian way of life. The purpose of the Sunday school is not merely to impart knowledge, but rather to teach a way of life. In Sunday school we learn that a Christian is a follower of Christ. Sunday school is not only a place where we learn about Jesus; it is a place where the Jesus way of life is actually being lived.

There was a man who carried a small picture of Christ in his billfold. He lost that billfold, but a few days later received it in the mail with all the money in it still there. With it was a simple note from the finder which said, "When I first found this billfold, I fully intended to keep the money, but when I looked at that picture of Christ, I had to send it back." The Sunday school shows people the Lord Jesus Christ in such a clear and distinct way that they want to live as He would have them live.

We have many Christian denominations in America. There is some difference in our beliefs and opinions. But right here we need to make a very important point. One minister in Texas is Dr. Asbury Lenox. He tells of a man of a different faith and a different theology who came to his study to talk with him. They talked, but they seemed not to find many points of agreement. The man got up to go, and as he was walking out the door, he turned and said to Dr. Lenox, "Preacher, we can get together on Jesus." Christian people have different opinions about things, but somehow, all of us "can get together on Jesus."

An Evangelistic Agency

The Sunday school is an evangelistic agency of the church. There are many types of evangelism, but none as effective as the Sunday school. Not only does the Sunday school go out and find persons and bring them in, it makes them a part of a Christian fellowship, and it offers definite Christian teaching and inspiration. We do not see many passenger trains today, but there is an old story that makes a good point. A train conductor was making his last run before he retired. Someone asked him how he felt about retiring. He made a beautiful reply: "It seems as if I have spent my life trying to help people get home." Really, that is the purpose of the Sunday school. We believe in living the Christian life on earth, and we also believe there is a life beyond this life. The Sunday school gives people purpose for living, as well as a destination for life.

One of the most fertile evangelistic fields of any church is its own church roll. It is so easy to take a roll and mark off persons who are not coming. It is much harder to go out and find them and win them back. Also let us keep reminding ourselves that two out of every three people in America today do not attend any church. Truly, ". . . the fields . . . are white already to harvest" (John 4:35). There are many persons who would like to belong to the fellowship of a Sunday-school class, if only some friendly person would invite them. Evangelism is a high-priority item of the Sunday school.

Church Doctrine and History

The doctrine and history of the church should be taught. Members should learn how the Christian church began and how their own denominational church began. They need to know exactly what a Christian believes and how the denomination to which they belong interprets and expresses that belief.

The great doctrines of the church are fundamental and essential, and without them there would be no church. The Sunday school has the responsibility, along with the pulpit, of teaching persons what is believed in its church.

Missions

An emphasis on missions, or outreach, as some would say, is a very necessary part of the teachings of the Sunday school. Our Lord said, ". . . Go ye into all the world. . . ." Some of us remember that when we were children in Sunday school we had what we called mite boxes. They referred to the widow's mite that Jesus talked about (Mark 12:42). Hers was a very small gift, but Jesus took note of it. As children, we were encouraged to put our pennies in the mite box, and then on a certain day they were brought to Sunday school and opened, and they were presented as missionary offerings. It was a tremendous lesson in missions.

The Sunday school has always been a prime mover of the church to be missionary minded, to reach out and help others. Many Sunday-school classes support special mission projects, and this is certainly to be commended. Many carry on service projects, working with persons in need. The Sunday school which is not missionary minded is not living up to the Great Commission of our Lord. We need to remember that the church *is* mission.

Prayer

Prayer is another one of the teachings of the Sunday school. For the child, prayer comes normally and naturally. This should be encouraged and enlarged as the child grows. We recall that the disciples said to Jesus, ". . . Lord, teach us to pray . . ." (Luke 11:1). This is the only thing the disciples ever asked Jesus to teach them. They never asked Him to teach them to preach, to work miracles, to build churches, or even to win the world. Somehow they realized that if they learned to pray, all these other things should come.

In response to their request, Jesus gave them what we call the Lord's Prayer. It is found in the sixth chapter of Saint Matthew's Gospel. The Lord's Prayer can be read in seconds, but one can study it for a lifetime. Teaching the principles and precepts of prayer is a major responsibility of the Sunday school.

Worship

Worship is one of the foundations of any religion, and this is one of the major responsibilities both for teaching and for practice in the Sunday school. To come to a moment of truth, or one of wonder and awe, about God, or Jesus, or the Christian way of life, is to experience worship. This often happens in Sunday school. In addition, as we have noted, members of the Sunday school must be encouraged to participate in the worship services of the church in the sanctuary. Really, the Sunday school and the worship service are two wings of the same bird. If the bird is to fly, it must use both of its wings; likewise, if the church is to develop, it must both teach and worship. The spirit of worship must undergird all the teachings of the church. In every Sunday-school class there should be symbols of worship, and the principles of worship should be taught.

Brother Lawrence said it best: "Practice the presence of God." Every Sunday-school class session should be a worship experience. Having a sense of awe and wonder about God is worship. Finding a new truth causes us to feel worshipful. It has been said, "Sometimes God puts us on our backs in order to give us a chance to look up." The theology of that statement is debatable, but it is not debatable that one of the reasons we bring people into a Sunday-school classroom is to inspire them to look up.

Stewardship

Stewardship is another one of the responsibilities of the Sunday school. In the four Gospels, Jesus is quoted as saying more about stewardship than He did about God, salvation, heaven, or any other subject. It is very important for little children to bring an offering to Sunday school. The giving of that offering during the class session should be a very special moment. The child should be taught that he or she is giving some of his or her money for God's work. This is one of the teachings that must be constantly held up before the people of the church. The truth is that, in most churches, when it comes to giving, we have written a rather sorry record. The average per capita giving in most churches is very low.

We need to teach that all we have belongs to God. There is a story of a man who pointed to a vast and fertile field of land to which he held title. He said to his minister, "To whom does this land belong?" The minister made a very wise reply. He said, "Ask me that question again a hundred years from now." It is a fact that none of us really owns anything. God allows us to be the stewards of certain of His possessions while we live on this earth. In our Sunday school we need to be taught stewardship accountability. This is a major part of the lesson.

Social Action

Social action and service are two more of the teaching responsibilities of the Sunday school. In the very first Book of the Bible the question is asked, ". . . Am I my brother's keeper?" (Genesis 4:9.) The answer to that question is emphatically *yes*. We are responsible for each other. We have social obligations. In the Sunday school we need to acquaint ourselves with the major social issues of our day. Alcohol is thought by many to be the worst problem in our society today. On the front page of the major newspaper in one of our American cities was the statement, "In this city there are 11,000 alcoholics. . . ." If that had been the end of the sentence, it would have been a statement of tremendous import, but the entire sentence was this, "In this city there are 11,000 alcoholics between the ages of eleven and fourteen years old." That statement is so shocking it is almost unbelievable. Surely the Sunday school must be concerned about that problem. There are other social problems, such as drugs, indecent literature, gambling, racial intolerance, housing conditions, and so on.

The social Gospel is never to take the place of the personal Gospel. We need to emphasize, however, that Jesus taught us to pray, "Thy kingdom come . . . . in earth. . . ." We believe that our churches can be colonies of heaven. We believe that we can have an impact on our society. We believe that we have social responsibilities.

World hunger is a grim statistic which we would like to avoid. But it is here and has its roots in complex forces. The church should feel responsible for educating its people in the conservation of life and resources—for removing exploitation and abuse. It should educate toward the living of a more simple life.

Not only are we citizens of the kingdom of God, we also are citizens of the communities in which we live. Christian

Education is involved in teaching about responsible citizenship. Every Sunday-school class or clusters of classes ought to have some definite social-action project. There are so many families in a city that need to be fed. There are so many institutions that need special support. Let the class do something to help make a better world.

World Peace

If we could pray only one prayer, what would that prayer be? For most of us it would be, "Lord, let us have peace on earth." What a blessing if we could know that there would never be another war! The human and physical resources which have been wasted in war could have been such a great blessing to humanity. If we could eliminate war, we would then be able to eliminate all the poverty of this world. In the Sunday school we teach peace with God, peace with ourselves, peace in our homes, peace in our society, and peace in our world. We cannot live isolated, just in our own nation. We are a part of all the earth. Certainly the Sunday school is a place where we learn to live and work together and project that spirit unto the uttermost parts of the earth. We need to teach and work for global justice.

These are just some of the responsibilities of our teaching in Sunday school. If these and other great lessons can be taught, learned, and put into practice, the future of our churches and of our society is undergirded.

For You to Do

Let the leaders of the Sunday school meet together and lift up such questions as:

1. Does our church teach the Bible?
2. What does it mean when we say, "Living the Christian life"?

3. Does the Sunday school really change attitudes and lives?

4. Are we experiencing the meanings we talk about?

5. What do our people know about the doctrines of our own church?

6. What are some of the obligations and duties of a citizen of our community?

7. What is the per-capita giving of our congregation?

These and other questions can be very provocative and excite us to the real possibilities of the Sunday school. Such a Sunday school will not only grow in attendance, but it will grow in power and effectiveness in the lives of the people, the community, and the entire world. Let us not belittle Christian Education.

13

Don't Just Teach the Bible—Teach Persons

In these pages we say a great deal about teaching the Bible: the Word of God. The Bible is our textbook, but we need to emphasize that, as important as knowledge of the Bible is, changing human lives is more important. The highest purpose of the Sunday school is to impart knowledge that results in life-changing experiences. But we need to emphasize the fact that just imparting knowledge is not enough. Changing persons is what it is all about.

The very title of this book, *How to Increase Sunday-School Attendance,* emphasizes the fact that we are concerned with numbers. Too often we have heard statements to the effect that we are not concerned about numbers; we are concerned about growing spiritually. Let us emphasize that any class which obtains spiritual growth will also obtain growth in numbers. It has often been said, "Religion is caught, not taught." That statement is only partly true. Much of our faith is taught, but, first, persons are drawn to Christ through the influence and lives of other persons who know Christ in such a way that they make Him attractive and winsome.

When lives are being changed, homes are being strengthened, marriages being made more meaningful, families learning how to live together in greater harmony, weaknesses in individuals overcome, persons experiencing

Jesus Christ as their Saviour and Lord and Friend, results such as these attract other people, and numerical growth is the normal result. We emphasize that spiritual growth and numerical growth go hand in hand. You cannot have one without the other.

The Purpose

We need to reemphasize the purpose of the Sunday school. It is simply to give to persons a growing experience in the Christian faith. This comes through teaching of God's Word, through loving fellowship with each other, and through the inspiration that we find in being in God's House together. Again we say, as important as it is to teach the Bible, Church history, social ethics, and all the other things that we do teach, the purpose of the Sunday school is to change human lives. That means that some whom even we consider to be good teachers are really missing the mark. A teacher might present a magnificent lecture without that lecture making any difference in the lives of the persons who hear it. There always must be two criteria by which we measure effectiveness in teaching: One is what is taught, and the other is what difference it makes in the lives of those who hear.

Somewhere we heard of a teacher in a certain Sunday school who proudly told the pastor he was spending an average of ten hours every week in preparation for the teaching of the class. This teacher went on to say that those ten hours were as much time as he had to spare in preparation for the class. The pastor was very wise and understanding. He suggested to the teacher that, for a few weeks, instead of spending ten hours in preparing the lesson, he might spend five hours in preparation and the other five hours in contacting new members of the class, either in personal visits or on the telephone. During these contacts, he could express interest in the person, ask about the person's problems and needs, and just get better acquainted with the person. More importantly, he could let that person know that he, as the teacher, was interested in that person's life and that he was praying in a special way for his or her needs.

In this particular case, we know that dramatic results followed. The teacher became even more effective, with half the amount of preparation. It was the inner reaction within the lives of the people that made a tremendous difference. Members of a class will be interested in what the teacher says, but they will be much more interested if they know that the teacher knows them and is concerned about them as persons. A loving, caring teacher gets dramatic results.

We certainly do not mean to minimize the fact that we need to constantly work to have better-prepared teachers, better teaching material, and better classroom facilities. But you can have all these things and have declining attendance. That has been proven in Sunday school after Sunday school across the land. It must be emphasized that all our teaching and preparation and facilities are for the purpose of helping people. Two phrases must always be kept in mind: "What does the Bible say?" and "How does it apply to the needs and problems of my life?" Persons are interested in what God said, but they are also interested in solutions to the problems of their lives.

Class members do not want to be told merely, "God is the answer." They want to know *how* God is the answer to such problems as disappointments in their job, a son or daughter who has missed the way, how to live with a non-Christian husband or wife, what to do about debts that seem more than can be paid, how to handle the racial conflict with which they may be faced, and so on. More teenagers than we know about are concerned to know what to do about or how to live with an alcoholic father or mother, or how to live in a home where both the father and mother work and nobody has any time for them, or which direction their lives ought to take, and the list could go on endlessly.

God does have the answers; however, it is the business of the teacher to know the questions. Many times we give answers to questions that nobody is asking. A lesson on how the walls of Jericho fell down can be very exciting, except it may not mean anything to the people who feel shut in by walls of life today. It is great to study the missionary journeys of Saint Paul, but many persons are seeking guidance for their own life's journey.

It is a very provocative thought to consider what our major task is. Look at the two following questions: Is it our task to bring God's Word to people? Is it our task to bring people to God's Word? The point is: We need to remember that the Sunday-school class, and everything that goes on in that class, is for the purpose of bringing people to God, changing lives, saving souls, answering life's problems, giving inspiration for living. We use God's Word to accomplish these purposes, but we need always to keep the purposes in mind.

Group Oneness

There are many ways to conduct classes, and each of those ways is good and has some merit. Some strictly use the lecture method, and others use questions and answers; but the class is not a group of individuals meeting in a room. Rather is it a group of persons who feel a oneness with one another, and in interacting with one another they find strength and inspiration. Class members need opportunities to know one another not only, as has been often said, to pray together, but also to play together. We need to apply the familiar phrase, "All work and no play makes Jack a dull boy." Our Sunday-school class must have social hours and opportunities to form friendships. We miss the mark when we allow a class to be just a group of individuals meeting in the same room. They need to share their experiences, to ask each other questions, to express their feelings.

Many classes feel that it is well worth the effort and cost to have a coffeepot, and maybe even doughnuts, around which the class members may enjoy a relaxed time together during the first few minutes of the class period.

We have not written at length about class socials and activities, but we certainly want to emphasize that we believe in their importance. Many members of a class have found a weekend retreat to be a life-changing experience. Socials are important and should be regularly and carefully planned.

Let us emphasize that in our Sunday school we teach the Word of God with the purpose of changing and strengthening human lives.

Appendix A

A Letter to Church Members

Here is a letter one pastor wrote to each church member who was not a member of the Sunday school.

Dear Church Member:

You are a member of _____ Church. Right now
(name)

we need your help. *Will you help us?* We are organizing some new Sunday-school classes and enlarging some others. Enclosed is a card listing the name and location of the class we want you to be a member of. Your presence will help get the class started. We already have a teacher, a president, and a secretary for each class.

The date the class starts is _____ . The time is
(date)

_____ A.M. *Will you come?*
(time)

Let me give you ten reasons for coming:

1. I would count your coming as a personal favor—so would the teacher, the officers of the class, and the other members of the class. The fact that so many of us want you to come is important.

2. Your coming would be an example and inspiration to

others, so your coming would be a favor to your church. Once there was a deaf man who went to church every Sunday. Someone asked why he went, since he could not hear anything. He replied, "My being there lets people know whose side I am on."

3. Fellowship with others is another reason to come. In a church we often make our best friends in a Sunday-school class. In times of both sorrow and joy, we share with each other. In a class we become members "one of another." (*See* Romans 12:5). In a class we will gain new friends, and all of us can use some more good friends.

4. In a Sunday-school class, you become more a part of the church. You become known and recognized by more people. Once a man was trying to carry a mattress up the stairs. He said, "I could carry it up, if I could just get a hold on it." In a class, you get a better hold on the church.

5. Membership in a Sunday-school class gives each of us more opportunity for leadership and influence in the church. It makes our church membership more meaningful; it makes our church stronger.

6. In a class, we study the Christian faith and life. Saint Paul said, "Study to shew thyself approved unto God, a workman that needeth not to be ashamed, rightly dividing the word of truth" (2 Timothy 2:15). In a class we learn more about the Christian beliefs and what we ought to do in our lives. The Bible is the foundation of all our study.

7. As a member of a class, you have opportunity to express your own thoughts and opinions. You have something to say that needs to be said. In your life you have learned much. By sharing your own experiences, you help others.

8. Every class should have some service projects. The Bible says, ". . . be ye doers of the word, and not hearers only . . ." (James 1:22). In a class we have opportunity to join with others in worthwhile service in the name of Christ.

9. There is an old saying, "All work and no play makes Jack a dull boy." We encourage each class to have some good times together: festive dinners, parties, and other recreational activities. There is another old saying, "Those who play together stay together." Being a member of a class can also be fun.

10. The Sunday school strengthens the church. We have a great church, located in the downtown center of the fastest-growing city in America. Nearly all the other downtown churches have fled to the suburbs. Our church has stayed and—with your help—will not only continue to stay, but will keep growing. However, our church must have a strong, growing Sunday school, and we need your help.

Here are ten reasons for your coming on _____ and being a part of this new class. Of
    (date)
course, if you happen to be out of town or sick that Sunday, you can come the next Sunday or the Sunday after that. Anyway, don't you think these are ten good reasons? Are they good enough reasons to cause you to come?

So we are asking *you* to come and be a member of a class. Bring the enclosed card so you will know exactly which class you are now a member of.

I want you to come for all the reasons stated above, but, again, I say your being here will be to me a personal favor, and I love you for coming.

Most cordially yours,
PASTOR

Enclosed Card:

```
Class: _____

Location: _____

        "Members One of Another"

            Romans 12:5

              Church

              Address

City, State, Zip Code
```

For You to Do

1. If the above letter appeals to you, use it above your signature.

2. Build on the idea of the letter and write your own.

Appendix B

Ten Commandments for Sunday-Morning Adult Groups

The people called the church are called to seek responsibly to understand the nature of God, how His will enters human history, and how His love calls us to live. This involves revelation in and through Jesus Christ, the Bible, and persons both past and present. We need to know what our human situation is and to be actively engaged in response to God's initiative in our lives. There should be an aliveness, an extraordinariness about us and about the groups in which we participate!

1. Maintain a Roll. Each of us wants to have a name and be known by it. Even a family has a roll: Husband and wife are recorded on church records and county and state records; children are given names and duly recorded in like manner. Families often write their roll in the Bible, the most sacred book in the household. The Bible makes it clear that to have a name is one of the most important parts of one's creation. To have a Sunday-morning-group roll is to care about the persons who come to the group and to affirm the infinite variety of God's creative power.

Enrollment of a person should include full name, address, and phone number. It should give the person's church affiliation and names of other family members, where applicable. The birth date should be recorded. Our enrollment cards ask for business identification. A note about hobbies and interests would be helpful. A name on a roll indicates that one is a member of that group. Each group should keep the information on each person up-to-date and pass the updated information on to the central office. The information is to be used for the person's best interest.

2. *Check the Roll Every Sunday*.   An expectation of group members is that they will come together every Sunday morning. Absence could mean lack of identity with the group, lack of interest in current study, illness, or normal activity away from the group. Knowing who is absent, and why, is very important. Knowing who is present is important, too. Knowing that your name is noted and recorded by someone is psychologically rewarding to one's sense of being.

Groups should use creative ways of checking the rolls from time to time. Most often, it will be done in a quiet, unobtrusive way.

3. *Follow Up on Absentees*.   Formulate a plan for doing this on a 100 percent basis. If you need a scriptural basis for this, remember the story Jesus told about the shepherd and sheep. To begin with, the story does not say the shepherd had "some sheep," nor a "large number of sheep," nor a "group of sheep." It says he had 100 sheep. He knew exactly how many sheep were in his flock. He had a flock roll.

Each night he checked his roll. He did not just look over the flock and say, "There are a good number present," or, "Most of us are here." Instead he knew exactly who was present and who was absent. He counted ninety-nine.

Then he followed up on that absentee. He did not say, "I hope that sheep will come back sometime." That very

night he went after that absent sheep, and he stayed after
it until he found it.

When a person knows he is missed, he is reminded you
care for him. Care should be taken not to nag the person
about his absence, but rather he should be given the loving
explanation, "We missed you. We need you. We want you
to be with us next Sunday." The reason for his absence
may call for a supportive gesture from you. Follow-up may
be done by phone, mail, or personal visitation. Spread the
follow-up among group members. However, someone
needs to be initially responsible.

4. Do Something About Visitors.   Some visitors will approach a class. Others need to be cultivated or invited.
After you get the visitors, make them feel at home with
you. The Christian community is never a closed community. Its nature is to reach out, to make welcome, to include. Have registration forms to help each group know
the visitors and follow up on them. Make sure each person
is recognized in an acceptable way and that someone has
the responsibility to follow through on him.

Sunday-morning groups provide a means for persons to
get to know other church members in a meaningful way.
Established group members should know that their actions
speak louder than any words. Does it really matter that a
newcomer or a guest feels a part of your church family? Or
do you leave all but the brave on the outside looking in,
probably to walk on down the road, maybe assuming all
church families are uncaring.

It is visitors who become members. Invite each one to do
so, or help him to find the right group. The director of
Christian Education and other church officers are eager to
help place persons in the best place.

5. Use Imagination in Room Setting.   Groups are assigned
spaces on a yearly basis, or sometimes less. The needs of all
groups, their sizes, formats, and so on are kept in mind

and the available spaces used to best advantage for everyone.

Each group should make its space tastefully attractive. Just as a house is important to a family and will reflect the personalities within it, so is a room to a class. Such things as carefully selected wall pictures, banners, group activity snapshots, and posters will add to the attractiveness and friendliness of a room. Careful thought should be given to the arrangement of chairs, use of tables, place for the teacher or leader in relation to the class. Chalkboards, bulletin boards, maps, and special equipment such as record players, projectors, and tape recorders are part of the setting. They should be used to best advantage. Thoughtful consideration about how visitors will be greeted will determine where the registration table is placed. Coffee service should be attended to. Literature and other resources should be made attractively available. Outdated notices, clutter, and literature should be removed.

So that everybody's business will not become nobody's business, there should be an understanding as to how these items will be handled. There are persons in each group who enjoy a variety of things. Having a responsibility makes one feel more a part of the group.

6. *Strictly Observe the Starting and Stopping Times.* There are a variety of things to be attended to within the Sunday-morning hour, in fact, so many that some groups will hold certain business items for weekday or weeknight meetings. Extended socializing will perhaps be planned at other times.

Individuals will feel more relaxed if the formal starting and stopping time is observed. A class timekeeper who is courteous but firm could be helpful. We know the worship service in the sanctuary begins and stops at certain times. We can depend on that. We plan around it. We know we must get there at a certain time and stay a certain length of time in order to participate fully. We know we will be released at a certain time so that we may move on to our next interest or responsibility, such as getting a child from the nursery. So it is with an adult group meeting on Sunday morning.

7. *Make the Sunday-Morning-Group Time Meaningful.* Take time to know the interests of the group members. Select teachers, leaders, and resources which will meet these needs, keeping in mind the overall purpose of church education, as stated in the beginning. Also keep in mind that no one group belongs to itself, but each is a part of a network of groups, and that teachers and resources are selected in agreement with the proper supervising bodies. Not just anyone may be selected to teach, nor may just any material be used.

Carefully elect officers who will lead the entire group in being involved. Then cooperatively work at doing the best you can. *Everyone* is a leader, a learner, and a teacher, but some must take specific responsibilities.

Joyfully express your feeling of love and affection within your group. This may be the only family some persons have. Real needs for friendship and belonging may not have been met elsewhere. This could be the most meaningful thread within your tapestry.

Many persons have searching questions about God, Jesus, the Bible, the church, Providence, who they are as persons, how to put Christian principles into actuality. The class format and the method of teaching should deal deeply and realistically with these questions. Leadership training is made available to enable these things to happen.

There are exciting things to learn, and learning is for all of life. We learn about the things which are significant to us. Group time is more meaningful if everyone becomes excited about learning and does some of the brainwork necessary for it. Teachers can do much to motivate a group toward this.

A variety of teaching methods and types of presentations will add spice to the pudding. Small groups within the larger group give each person an opportunity to express himself. A presentation might be made in the form of a panel, symposium, debate, film, chalk-talk, and so on. It is a measurable fact that more learning takes place when there is group involvement. The lecture, or verbal explanation of information, is more effective when there is an opportunity for feedback. It is not by chance that the most effective counselors listen more than they talk; so it is with the skilled leader who wants to help persons grow. When members become motivated to study and talk beyond group time, you know significant things are happening.

Evaluate where you are from time to time. Set goals to make things happen. Witness about God's gifts to you.

8. Provide Fellowship Opportunities.   The word *fellowship* has sometimes been misused to mean only informal talking together or having coffee together. The deepest kind of fellowship exists when a group does a meaningful project together, worships together, or struggles through to a significant intellectual or emotional discovery. But playing together is equally important. Weekday parties and activities are essential in maintaining class spirit. This additional time is needed by most groups. Having informal fun together makes it easier to study and pray together. It is in such times that persons may get to talk with each other about their other-than-Sunday life.

9. Do All the Good You Can.   Within the group, develop genuine concern for each other, but also reach out in service. Be good for something. Each group should have at least one project to do together; many will have more. Your church office can help you know about projects to do so that you may evaluate the desirability of your group getting involved in them.

Some opportunities for service are hospitals, homes for
the aged, shut-ins of the church, court volunteers, teaching children or youth, sewing, serving food, and so on.
Giving money to worthy causes is one way groups may
help. The money may be used to buy Bibles or other resources. It could be used to pay for a hospital bed for a sick
person. There are a thousand ways it may be used. Groups
need to realize, however, that their members also contribute to the overall budget of the church, where the overall
ministry is carried out.

When we take our response to our faith seriously, we
become a sent people. Many things we will do individually.
But some things we need to do as a group.

10. Be a Part of the Whole Church. The church is
people—a particular people. _____ Church located at
_____ any town or community, any state, United States of
America, Earth, is part of the Church Universal.

Each group within _____ Church is a part of the whole
church and should take care to not be apart from it.

In the areas of curriculum, leadership, structure,
teachers, projects, and so on, coordination, help, and direction are given through the education staff and officers.
Each group should recognize its need to relate to this.

Although Sunday-morning groups provide prime time
for maximum adult participation, there are other programs which provide opportunities. These must be coor-
dinated and planned so that they are supportive and helpful. A class should recognize its need to participate in the
worship services of the congregation. A group can encourage individual attendance. Sometimes it might go as a
group. If one substitutes class time for worship in the
sanctuary, then the class does not understand its purpose,
or the purpose of worship. The group is made stronger
confessing our less-than-God-ness, seeking the kingdom

together, asking forgiveness within the gathered community, hearing the proclaimed Word, and going through the ritualistic ceremonies which have deeply embodied meanings—all these give us strength and vision. Our group time is an extension of this, but at the same time an input into it. In the group we dig into meanings and establish one-to-one relationships which enable us to live out our beliefs.

Think of the church as the body of Christ. Think of your own body. When you hurt even a finger, the whole body is aware of it and feels the pain. Each part of the body is unique but important to the whole. So it is with the church.

For You to Do

1. Use this appendix as a study for adult classes or the education committee.

2. Write your own Ten Commandments.

Appendix C

What Makes Them Grow? Principles We Have Observed in Growing Sunday Schools

We do not necessarily approve or disapprove of each of these statements. We are only reporting our observations.

Plan it big—keep it simple.

Go after parents; they will bring the children.

A church which limits its growth begins a program of self-destruction.

The largest Sunday schools in America are city wide. There is no need to limit your church to one neighborhood.

The church which is not interested in numbers will not have them.

In many large Sunday schools, small class groupings and the Board of Christian Education are eliminated. Large classes are taught by skilled teachers and motivators, and the Sunday school is administered by professionals.

Some believe that any dedicated, growing Christian who studies the Bible and loves people can teach a Sunday-school class, and people will respond.

Godly jealousy is the secret for church growth: "jealous for souls and jealous for God."

Personal visitation, letter writing, telephoning, and other contacts are essential in winning people. Advertising does not get people to church and Sunday school, but advertising helps the individual win others.

People are more apt to go where they can find a suitable place to park.

People enjoy being in a full room. A crowded room gives the impression that this is where the action is. Successful small classes do not meet in large rooms.

Successful Sunday schools push every week, but they have four to six major pushes throughout the year.

Some churches have found that busing was too expensive. They have tried a promotion campaign at the same time they eliminated busing and found that the people responded by driving their own cars or seeking public transportation. In some instances, they even experienced an increase in attendance.

A successful Sunday-school teacher said, "I did not write the Bible; I just teach it."

We know of several churches which have simultaneous worship services in their buildings. In one area there is a traditional service, in another area a contemporary service, and in another area perhaps a charismatic service, and so on. The idea is that different personalities or modes of worship attract different people.

Sometimes a Sunday school can get so involved in organization that it forgets teaching and evangelism.

A church does not grow through Christian education; it grows through evangelism. Teaching follows winning.

Successful Sunday schools study the difficult Sundays—
that is, the Sundays that pull down attendance averages—
such as the various holidays. Instead of surrendering to
smaller attendance, special promotions should be planned
for difficult Sundays.

Some churches have a regular Saturday-night youth
service at the church.

Successful Sunday schools give specific attention to each
age. One program does not meet the need of all age
groups.

Some of the most successful Sunday schools are the responsibility of staff members instead of lay groups. Some
feel that professional staff members can make better decisions than a board of Christian Education.

Other successful Sunday schools believe that the more
persons who are involved in the decision process, the
stronger the Sunday school is. Therefore, many persons
are involved in many committees and boards.

Many successful Sunday schools use a Wednesday-night
meeting to instill loyalty and passion into their Sunday-
school teachers and staff.

In the words of Winston Churchill, some Sunday-school
leaders say that the three reasons for their success are:
"Blood, sweat, and tears."

Some Sunday schools have no separate class treasuries.
All offerings in the class go into the general church funds.

When a new member joins, some classes have that
member pledge to support the class with his prayers, his
presence, his gifts, and his services. Some classes ask each
new member to promise to talk to at least one person each
week about God.

We know of one large Sunday school which reports that 75 percent of its members are tithers.

It is possible for a pastor to be jealous of the Sunday school in his church, preferring that his church be known as a great preaching center. The truth is, Sunday school and the church service are never competitors, but wings of the same bird.

Many successful churches believe that the secret of Sunday-school growth is regular teacher training.

The growing Sunday school is the one that reaches young married couples.

Some churches emphasize recreational facilities, believing that the human body is the temple of the Holy Spirit and that the church must minister to the whole person.

Every time they preach, many preachers preach for decisions.

Some Christian educators believe that enrollment is more important than attendance. They feel that if people are committed to the Sunday school by enrollment, attendance will automatically follow. Thus, some churches list enrollment figures instead of attendance.

Sometimes the criticism is made that a person gets lost in a big church. But many big churches have better staffs and better facilities and do a better job with keeping up with their members than do small churches.

The staff of a church belongs to the pastor and is responsible to him or her. The pastor is responsible to the church. This is the belief of many successful churches.

Too many cooks in the kitchen can spoil the dinner. And too many persons involved in the administration of the Sunday school can spoil the program. This is the belief of some very successful Sunday schools.

All unusually successful Sunday schools which we observed had regular programs of personal visitation.

It has been well said, "You cannot build a Sunday school without music, but neither can you build one on music."

Some Sunday schools believe strongly in small, closely graded classes. Others believe in what they call the master teacher, that is, a few very large classes. We observe that either method can be used successfully.

We observe that unusually successful churches and Sunday schools have both strong pastoral leadership and strong lay leadership. Both are required for the greatest success.

One pastor said it this way, "My leadership would be totally ineffective without the confidence of my people. Therefore, I must conduct my life and my ministry in such a way as to never jeopardize the confidence of one person in my church."

It might be a good idea for each Sunday school to have its own hall of fame. Persons in the church could be nominated, and being elected would be a supreme honor and inspiration to others to render dedicated service.

There are those who say that the biblical text for a great Sunday school is Acts 5:42. "And daily in the temple, and in every house, they ceased not to teach and preach Jesus Christ."

One successful minister put it this way, "The lay persons in the church are busy all day long about their own business. A small group of them should not expect to meet briefly one night a month and tell the pastor and staff how to run the church. The lay persons should trust the leadership of the pastor and staff."

Most successful churches have both a past and a potential.

A large church we know believes strongly in setting goals for each and every department and for financial income. Each week goals and results are printed in the church paper.

One church has a four-point program: 1. Win them. 2. Teach them. 3. Make witnesses of them. 4. Lead them in worship.

God builds His work around human personalities.

Just because a church is small does not mean that it cannot effectively and successfully apply the principles of a large church.

We have observed no church with a growing Sunday school in which the senior pastor did not personally give active leadership.

We have observed no growing Sunday school in any church which does not have a strong pulpit ministry.

We have observed that a strong choir is extremely supportive of the entire church program.

In a growing church and Sunday school which is centered around a dynamic personality, it is sometimes wondered what will happen when that personality leaves or retires or dies. We observe that ". . . sufficient unto the day is the evil thereof" (Matthew 6:34). Tomorrow will take care of itself.

"I felt the members of that church really wanted me." That sentence, and variations of it, is the key to growth in any Sunday school.

If a church ever decides it is too big, it begins a program of self-destruction.

An effective, paid staff member pays his or her own way. We observed that many churches are understaffed. Some pastors and churches are too reluctant to hire persons to perform special tasks.

Growing churches believe in the importance of the organized, institutional church.

There is not a conflict in emphasizing quality and numbers. One supports the other, and both should be emphasized. In the Lord's work big is not bad. Churches that grow are bold in their promotion and advertising.